You Can't Make Me Angry

You Can't Make Me Angry

By Dr. Paul O.

Capizon Publishing

You Can't Make Me Angry
Copyright © 1999 by Dr. Paul O.

Publication of this work does not imply affiliation with, approval of or endorsement by Alcoholics Anonymous World Services, Inc.

The ideas and suggestions in the book are intended to supplement, not replace any needed advice of trained professionals. The author and publisher disclaim any liability arising directly or indirectly from the use of this book.

Cover design and photo by Capizon Publishing.

Publisher's Cataloging in Publication
O., Paul (1918 -2000)
You Can't Make Me Angry / by Dr. Paul. O.
___p. ___cm
ISBN: 978-0-9659672-1-1
1. Alcoholism—Psychological aspects. 2. Alcoholism—Family relationships. 3. Twelve-step programs
HV5278   362.2918   LCCN: 2002102547

Printed in the USA on acid-free paper.

Capizon Publishing   www.capizon.com

Eleventh Printing December 2021

Contents

Acknowledgments

Thanks to everyone who made it possible for me to write this book. This includes of course all the members of Alcoholics Anonymous and Al-Anon with whom I have come in contact over the years.

Thanks specifically to Ira F. and Bob L. for their time and help with the editing. Special mention in this regard must go to Dick C. who, with his high tech equipment, provided both editing and encouragement in spite of the fact that he is legally blind.

Finally, I want to give special thanks to Sue M. for her long-term friendship, her encouragement and her extensive support.

Thanks also to everyone who deserves to be mentioned. Naming them all would make far too long a list.

Dr. Paul passed away in May of 2000, a few months after completing the manuscript for this book. He has probably been the secretary of a morning meeting somewhere in heaven ever since. His wife, Maxine, joined him there in July of 2001.

ANYONE can become angry—that is easy. But to be angry with the right person, to the right degree, at the right time, for the right purpose, and in the right way—that is not easy.

ARISTOTLE
The Nichomachean Ethics

Preface

I am an active member of both Alcoholics Anonymous and Al-Anon, and I occasionally attend meetings of other recovery programs. While this book is directed primarily at members of any of these organizations, non-members could also benefit. To this end, general information regarding the philosophy of A.A. and Al-Anon is included in the appendix.

Although the literature of A.A. and Al-Anon will occasionally be quoted (with permission), detailed suggestions for successfully living those two programs will not be included here. Neither is the information presented here meant to take the place of professional counseling and advice.

Except when specifically stated, all names are fictitious, and characters are composites of several individuals. A reader may at times identify with these and mistakenly assume they are the person being discussed. Such similarities are coincidental. The only exceptions are the stories by Naomi D., Elizabeth H., Judy R., Jane U. and Sue W. These individuals, at my request, graciously submitted their stories specifically for presentation here, and I am indeed grateful to them for this kindness.

One might suppose a person writing a book would know what they had to say and would proceed with saying it. In this case, that is only partially true. Earlier, when I wrote *There's More To Quitting Drinking Than Quitting Drinking*[1], I start-

---

[1] Dr. Paul O., *There's More To Quitting Drinking Than Quitting Drinking,* (Torrance CA: Capizon Publishing, 2001).

ed with only a general idea of what I had in mind. The more I wrote, the more I understood what I was trying to say. As I continued to write, I understood more and more what I believe, what I think, what I feel, and what is important to me. Writing clarified my thinking and allowed me to become more comfortable being me. I experienced both spiritual and emotional growth during the process. If I'm lucky, the same things will happen again this time. In addition, it is my sincere hope that the reader also will benefit as a result of reading this book.

In addition, earlier, and especially prior to my recovery from alcoholism, my behavior resulted in unhappiness and discomfort not only for me but also for a number of other people. By focusing on my emotional sobriety now, and by sharing my efforts with others, I hope to make what are known in A.A. as "living amends" both to myself and to those people, many of whom are now deceased.

So, if we're both lucky, I will grow and learn by writing, and you will profit by reading. In the Preface to her book, *Revolution From Within—A Book of Self-Esteem*[2], Gloria Steinem quoted Thomas Carlyle as having said, "The best effect of any book is that it excites the reader to self-activity." She ended by saying, "If you learn a tenth as much from this book as I have, I'll be a happy writer."

I agree with those statements.

Good Luck and Godspeed to both of us.

---

[2] Gloria Steinem, *Revolution From Within—A Book of Self-Esteem*, (Boston: Little, Brown & Co., 1992), p. 17.

1. THE PROBLEM

Who's writing this? At the time of this writing, I am 82 years of age and Maxine (better known as Max) and I have been married for 61 years. We hadn't planned on living this long, and we certainly hadn't expected to be married this long.

After I completed pharmacy school, Max and I worked my way through medical school. This was followed by thirty years in the private practice of internal medicine. Twenty of those years were devoted mainly to the treatment of alcoholism and other chemical dependencies. Since retirement, my primary interests have been writing, operating a small publishing business, and involvement in both Alcoholics Anonymous and Al-Anon.

When I was four years old, my father opened a home/drug store combination and I literally grew up in a drug store. My father was successful in that, with considerable difficulty, he survived the Great Depression. I remember him as having been admired by the people in that small community, but at home he was stern, serious, and often ill-tempered. He died rather abruptly when I was 16.

Sadly, I realize now that I am much like my father. Unless I monitor my mood, it drifts into one of irritability, crabbiness and depression. I have always been, at times, hard to live with. Since getting sober, I am no longer able to drink or use drugs. As a result, I've had to find better ways of dealing with my emotions.

With the recovery program I practice these days, the thought of taking a drink doesn't occur to me. I haven't had a drink since July 31, 1967. Yet I'm not even thirsty. Staying physically sober presents no particular problem for me. I'm amazed at how easy it is for me to accomplish today that which I found impossible before the program.

Emotional sobriety, on the other hand, presents quite a different problem. This requires considerably more of my focused attention. By explaining how I work at it and what I do to obtain and preserve it, I hope to clarify my thinking and become more proficient at maintaining this phase of my recovery. If nothing else, the effort spent writing this will help me focus my attention on this important subject.

I have been interested in this subject for a long time. Many years ago I saved a brief newspaper article about a man who purchased a paper ever day from a man who was habitually crabby and irritable. He did this without ever himself getting upset. When asked why or how he could do this, he answered, "Why should I allow that man to determine my mood for the day?"

That sentiment appealed to me then, and it appeals to me today. There's enough misery of my own making without taking on anyone else's.

Overview of the subject. Nothing that an insane or neurotic person feels, thinks or does is totally different from the feelings, thinking and behavior of a so-called "normal" person. The difference is only a matter of degree. We all daydream to some extent, but only the mentally ill actually live their lives in a fantasy world.

A paranoid schizophrenic, for instance, might tell you that someone is controlling their thinking by means of radio waves. They believe, therefore, that they are not responsible for their feelings, their thinking or their behavior. They insist they are under the control of someone else—some imaginary enemy.

Think about that for a moment. The feelings, thinking and behavior of psychotic individuals differs only in degree, quantity, intensity—not in quality or substance—from that of the rest of us. Add the fact that we so-called normal people *frequently* allow other people and situations to control our emotions (and thereby our thinking and behavior), and the difference between *us* and *them* begins to blur.

This surrendering of emotional control often gets alcoholics drunk. (Or at least serves as an excuse for drinking.) It also seriously detracts from the quality of life of non-alcoholics. And it is almost completely unnecessary.

Eleanor Roosevelt recognized this truth when she said, *No one can make you feel inferior without your consent*[1].

Not only can people not make you feel inferior, they can't make you feel any particular emotion unless you willingly accept their suggestion.

We declare our emotional independence when we refuse to allow others to dictate our emotional

---

[1] Eleanor Roosevelt, *This Is My Story* (New York: Harper & Brothers, 1937).

state—when we make our own decisions as to how we are going to feel at any particular moment. Emotional independence leads to emotional sobriety (peace of mind), and emotional sobriety is conducive to long-term physical sobriety. Physical sobriety in an alcoholic without emotional sobriety is often not only an unpleasant condition, it can lead to drinking (a so-called *slip*) or, in the absence of drinking, to what is referred to as a *dry drunk*—drinking behavior without drinking.

However, so-called *slips* and *dry drunks* are not limited to alcoholics. Al-Anon members are as prone to *slips* as are alcoholics, perhaps more so. They have what they refer to as a *slip* every time they become unduly upset with their children or their alcoholic spouse. When this inappropriate emotional state continues over a period of time, they can be said to be on a *dry drunk*. Although they are not drinking, they are thinking and behaving like a drinking alcoholic. They may, for instance, have tried to control another person or situation that is none of their business.

Father Barney, a Jesuit Priest who used to host retreats for alcoholics and their spouses, liked to compare the recovery process to a baseball diamond. He pictured physical sobriety as first base, mental sobriety as second base, emotional sobriety as third base and spiritual sobriety as home plate.

I like that analogy. I like breaking things into smaller parts. As for example, handling problems one day at a time as recommended in the Alcoholics Anonymous program. Once alcoholics get physically sober and pass first base, the problems they face are essentially those faced by Al-Anon members.

From that point on, both A.A. and Al-Anon members struggle toward the same goal—increasing their mental, emotional and spiritual sobriety.

During my drinking years, like many practicing alcoholics, I deluded myself with the thought that if you had my wife or my problems, you'd drink too. In my mind, people and situations "drove me to drink." Once I became sober, I had to learn to handle my emotions so these same people and situations could no longer do this to me.

In general, all alcoholics must maintain their emotional sobriety in order to comfortably maintain their physical sobriety. By the same token, recovering Al-Anon members must maintain their emotional sobriety in order to maintain their sanity. Neither can afford to let others control their emotions. Both must maintain their emotional independence in order to survive.

"It is a spiritual axiom that every time we are disturbed, no matter what the cause, there is something wrong *with us*." This statement appears in *Twelve Steps And Twelve Traditions*[2] published by Alcoholics Anonymous. "With us" appears in the original text in italics. Personally, I think it would have been appropriate to have also italicized "no matter what the cause." Regardless of the cause of our emotional disturbances, there is always something we can do about our feelings. In fact, we are the only one who can do something about them.

---

[2] *Twelve Steps And Twelve Traditions,* (New York: A.A.World Services, Inc., 1981), p. 90.

Accepting Responsibility. Usually, however, instead of accepting responsibility for my feelings, I do the opposite. I focus on trying to bring about a change in the offending person or situation. I blame my emotional state on what is happening outside me rather than admitting that at every moment of every day, consciously or unconsciously, I exercise a choice as to my mood and how I am going to feel.

A few years back, Max and I led a workshop on relationships. I shared with the group how I had given Max a written declaration of emotional independence stating that she was no longer responsible for my feelings. Thereafter, I could no longer tell her, "You made me angry," or "I feel bad and it's your fault because of what you did (or said)." I also explained how, as a corollary, I was no longer responsible for her feelings. We both agreed that from now on we are each responsible for our own feelings.

During the workshop discussion period, a middle-aged woman mentioned several times how poorly she and her husband were getting along. At one point he dropped by the meeting but refused to stay. She complained that she couldn't get him to talk. She also stressed how upset he became every time she tried to make him feel better. This occurred on the rare occasions when he did express a negative feeling. When he did so, she told him what he should do and how he ought to feel.

At the end of the session, she complained about how bad she felt when he verbalized a long list of things he didn't like about her. She told him how uncomfortable this made her feel, but he continued to do it anyway. She appeared quite sad and pitiful.

In my opinion, her husband's *passive-aggressive* behavior made obvious his secret desire to get back at her for belittling his feelings on the rare occasions when he did express them. Neither of these partners had the courage to accept responsibility for their own feelings. Both preferred to remain a victim of the other's behavior.

* * *

The Responsibility Statement, the motto of the International Alcoholics Anonymous Convention in 1965 states:

I am responsible . . .

When anyone, anywhere,
reaches out for help, I want
the hand of A.A. always to be there.
And for that: I am responsible.

This sounds quite noble. But, *as stated*, I think it doesn't make sense. A.A. can't possibly assume responsibility for every needy person throughout the world. It can accept responsibility for being there when anyone seeks help with a drinking problem, but it can't be there for every victim of flood, starvation, war, pestilence, abuse, persecution, and other disasters. Alcoholics Anonymous is not the Red Cross, and it can't support everyone everywhere who asks for every kind of help.

Many of us have a similar unrealistic sense of personal responsibility.

Precisely what in life are you personally responsible for? Just where does your responsibility begin and where does it end?

Ask yourself: If you were somehow forced to choose between the person you love most in life versus your personal happiness, which would you choose?

Anthony de Mello asks this question in his book *Awareness*[3]. He suggests that most people would unselfishly choose the person they love over their own personal happiness. Then he speculates as to what the relationship would be like with two people always choosing their partner's happiness over their own—that is, two always-unhappy people relating to each other!

On every commercial airline flight, before the plane takes off, specific instructions are given as to what to do in case of a sudden decompression. "The oxygen masks will drop down from the ceiling," we are told. "If you are sitting next to or near a small child, put on your own mask first, then the mask of the child."

Look out for yourself first. Otherwise you might both fail to survive.

A.A. members realize the importance of statements such as this when it comes to sobriety. They work what they call "a selfish program." They know that if they get drunk, nothing else matters. The Traditions of Alcoholics Anonymous carry this thought all the way to the group level. The Traditions state that the A.A. group is more important than the individual alcoholic. If the group disappears, so will the members.

---

[3] Anthony de Mello, *Awareness,* (New York: Doubleday), p. 9.

Every long-time, sober alcoholic knows that sobriety is extremely jealous. If the spouse, children, car, house, job, money, sex or anything else achieves greater importance to the alcoholic than his or her sobriety, sobriety leaves. It will not compete. It demands top priority in the alcoholic's life.

Geraldine M., for example, thoroughly enjoyed sobriety. She got a job. Soon she had a second job. In spite of all advice to the contrary, she decided to return to school. Work and school continued to grow in importance. Now she's trying to get sober again.

Every alcoholic with any length of sobriety realizes the preeminent importance of sobriety. It is the basis for A.A.'s slogan "First Things First," and for the admonition given newcomers to not become emotionally involved in the first year of recovery. Sobriety must come before everything else.

Indeed, when two alcoholics talk about an acquaintance who has had a slip, one of them commonly ends the conversation with, "It could have been worse. It could have been me," and the other responds with, "It could have been worse than that. It could have been me!"

Al-Anon   Alcoholics often don't appreciate this seemingly selfish attitude toward recovery when an Al-Anon member begins to look out for themselves as, for example, when they divorce the alcoholic or leave him or her at home while they go off to a meeting. The alcoholic feels abandoned and resentful in spite of the fact that we all have to look out for ourselves first.

Alcoholics also sometimes get upset when it is suggested that they might benefit by going to Al-Anon. They act like you said they don't belong in A.A. and should go to Al-Anon instead.

Referring to ". . . doctors, psychologists, and practitioners of various kinds," the Big Book of Alcoholics Anonymous[4] says, "Do not hesitate to take your health problems to such persons." Yet, when it is suggested that an alcoholic might get help for an interpersonal problem by attending Al-Anon meetings, their reaction often implies that a semi-adversarial relationship exists between the two programs, that a person can't successfully belong to both organizations at the same time. As far as I can determine, nothing in the literature of either organization supports such a view.

The two organizations compliment rather than compete with each other. Al-Anon members can learn a great deal by attending A.A. meetings. And my observation has been that we alcoholics, when we are willing, can also learn a great deal by attending Al-Anon meetings.

As I understand it, Alcoholics Anonymous believes alcoholism is an incurable, terminal disease, and the A.A. program of recovery is a spiritual way of life which allows alcoholics to live comfortably free from alcohol no matter what is or is not going on in their lives.

In like manner, Al-Anon is a spiritual way of life which allows Al-Anon members to live life comfortably and emotionally sober no matter what

---

[4] *Alcoholics Anonymous*, Third Edition, (New York: A.A. World Services, Inc., 1976), p. 133.

the alcoholic, or anyone else, is doing or not doing. In this sense, as mentioned earlier, it's more difficult to avoid a slip in Al-Anon than in Alcoholics Anonymous.

In daily life, the occasions for a possible Al-Anon slip are more common than the occasions for a slip in A.A. In this very precise sense, the Al-Anon program is more strict than the A.A. program. As already stated, A.A. helps alcoholics stay physically sober under any and all circumstances, while Al-Anon helps it's members stay emotionally sober whether the alcoholic is drinking or not.

It's a beautiful sight to watch alcoholics, especially two in a relationship, combine the teachings of both programs. By doing this, they arc able to stay sober and emotionally comfortable regardless of the behavior of their partner and of the other people in their lives. This requires a great deal of emotional independence.

Goals and values.   At the end of this next paragraph, stop reading long enough to think about yourself for a moment.

What do you value in life? Make a mental or preferably a written list of the things that are important to you. Now arrange the items in descending order of their importance. This is your own personal list. No one can arrange it for you.

Now, notice where on your list you've placed serenity, emotional sobriety, peace of mind— whatever you want to call it. How important is this to you? What comes before it on the list?

Many of us, without realizing what we are doing, routinely put a low value on our serenity, our emotional sobriety. Sometimes it is even awarded a negative value. At an Al-Anon meeting, a member admitted, "I get to feeling good; then I suddenly realize I shouldn't be feeling like this when there is so much trouble going on with my husband and my kids and the neighbors. I should be working on these things."

Many of us say that serenity and peace of mind are important to us. Our behavior, however, belies our words when we promptly discard our emotional sobriety at the slightest provocation provided by ridiculously unimportant people and events. For example, before recovery and early in sobriety I routinely threw my sobriety at other drivers on the freeway, people who didn't even want it. In fact, they didn't know they had it, until, by gestures, horn-blowing or erratic driving, I made them aware of how they had annoyed me! Many of us do things like this out of habit.

The trick is to become aware. Carry this thought of awareness a bit further. Ask yourself: What motivates you? Do you have a distinct goal or desire, or are you drifting, waiting for something or someone to motivate you? Are you waiting for your Higher Power to tell you what to do? Do you interpret "Easy does it" to mean doing nothing while waiting?

Who or what makes you happy or sad, confident or fearful, up-beat or worried? Do you choose your feelings, or does some other person or situation *make* you feel the way you feel?

What would your life be like if you had the courage and wisdom to take charge? What if you made up your mind that from now on for the rest of your life, you alone would decide how you were going to feel? What kind of emotional life would you choose for yourself?

You might start with the thought of who you are now. Write a paragraph describing yourself in such a way that if you were to read it, you would recognize it as you. If that's too much trouble, carefully pick one word that best describes your basic, overall personality—perhaps a word like happy, depressed, friendly, optimistic, unenthusiastic, fearful, loving, resentful, disappointed—whatever word fits best. If you can't decide, and you're willing to take the risk, ask several close acquaintances or relatives to do it for you.

Is that the person you want to be? Are you ready for a change, or are you in the victim role in that you can't change because some person or circumstance won't allow it? Is that *really* so, or do you like to think it's so?

Sue W. thought for sure her happiness was supposed to be controlled by others until she found the courage to change. Then she discovered that what she had thought wasn't true. An otherwise really sharp lady, it never occurred to her that she had the power to alter her life—by simply choosing to do so.

One night while trying to fix dinner, she called me sobbing because her husband had hurt her feelings again. In the past, her reaction to these episodes had always been the same, "I would put a smile on my face and serve him dinner."

I suggested that she might feel differently if she acted differently. When she could think of no possible way to change anything. I suggested that she might, for example, put the kids in the car and go out to dinner and a movie.

She insisted her husband would be furious if she did that, but to her surprise, and literally shaking with fear, she did it anyway. Later she told me, "That may sound like nothing to you, but it was a really big deal to me. It taught me autonomy and freedom and the fact that I am a human being with rights. It was my personal 'giant step for mankind'."

If the victim role is as unpleasant as Sue's story makes it sound, why is it so popular? For one thing, the victim role provides a sense of security by eliminating the need to change. It eliminates the need to even try. Furthermore, it provides a pleasant sense of superiority. Instead of feeling responsibility for myself, I feel powerful and superior to you as I point out to anyone who will listen what *you* are doing wrong. "You're the problem; you need help, not me"—or so we like to think when we are playing the role of victim.

Is it possible for us to maintain complete control of our emotional state at all times? That is, to not allow another person or situation to ever make us angry, sad, disappointed, depressed, fearful, or any other negative emotion? Definitely not.

Absolute, total, constant control is not possible and not even desirable. But we can make progress. With practice, a good attitude, and the help of a Higher Power, we can markedly reduce both the frequency and the duration of those periods when we allow others to determine the state of our emotions.

With increasing awareness of both how we feel at any particular moment, and why we have chosen to feel that way, we develop the ability to change our emotional state if we wish to do so. We generate an awareness of whether we have chosen our current feelings or have allowed them to be implanted by an outside person or circumstance. Having determined that, we are in a position to change them if we wish. First we must have the awareness, and the awareness must be followed by willingness. Only then can change take place.

People make such changes all the time. Mable S. has been an active member of Al-Anon for twenty years. She is consistently one of the happiest and most pleasant people I know. She maintains a good attitude in spite of her cantankerous husband's uncontrollable drinking for the past thirty years. Because of Al-Anon, Mable realizes that she is not a reflection of her husband's behavior. His behavior, on the other hand, is a reflection of a disease he did not ask to have. On a daily basis, she accepts those facts and stays busy making the best of her own life.

Helen M., a recovering alcoholic with three small children, works a good recovery program and stays sober and enthusiastic while living with a still-drinking alcoholic husband who persistently does everything he can to "drive her to drink." In spite of his shenanigans, she attends meetings regularly, talks on the phone, works with her sponsor and sponsees, practices both the A.A. and Al-Anon principles in her daily life, and generally maintains a healthy attitude.

Elizabeth H. told me, "When my ex-husband used to come home from work mad, I wouldn't let him take it out on me. I would say something like, 'I've had a really nice day so far, and I'm not willing to let go of it this way.' That worked so well I also used it with my sister who would attack without warning like a terrorist bomber. One day I just said to her, 'Hey, I called to wish you a happy day. I'll call back when you're in a better mood. Goodbye'."

Regarding emotional sobriety and not allowing others to control how she feels, Elizabeth said, "I think that is one of the hardest tasks I face every day. I remember when my daughter was active in her addiction, and my sponsor told me, 'The best thing you can do for her is to be okay yourself. We're going to let her join us in recovery; we're not going to join her in her disease.'"

There are thousands and thousands of examples of real-life heroes among the millions of members of A.A. and Al-Anon—people conducting themselves as the person God wants them to be in spite of the people, situations and circumstances that surround them.

Of course, not all heroes are in A.A. and Al-Anon. That's just where those of us in recovery see and learn to emulate them. With them as role models, we choose to be affected in positive rather than in undesirable, negative ways. Lacking sufficient courage ourselves, we borrow courage from courageous people and from our Higher Power, and it works.

Oddly enough, not everyone wants to be affected in a positive way. Some individuals are addicted to their negative feelings. Just as many drinking people place little value on physical sobriety and never get sober, so too, many of us place little value on our emotional sobriety and never get comfortable.

Pat J. thinks her husband doesn't appreciate how hard she works keeping house and raising four children, so she remains unhappy and complains constantly about how difficult life is. Men, too, sometimes feel sorry for themselves and act this way in an effort to get their family to appreciate all the work they do to support them.

John W. stays upset because his wife doesn't act right, his kids continually misbehave and create problems, and his health continues to deteriorate. Yet he makes no effort to change himself or anything else in any way. Any happiness that enters John's life stays only briefly.

Jane T. won't even allow happiness to enter her life. She used to call me almost daily, always with reasons why she couldn't be happy. Over and over she stated, "I've been like this all my life." She procrastinated endlessly every time I made a suggestion for change, and when I gave her the name of an inspirational book to read, she said she "had to stay sober first"—as if that were a reason to forever do nothing other than to just not drink.

Henry G. says he feels bad "half the time" which is about the way he "usually is." He says he was better for a period of time but has "slipped back into my old ways." He stopped going to meetings, and no longer follows his exercise program. He's read "just a little" of the three books I loaned him on self-esteem. Henry bought a set of four tapes on procrastination, and started to listen to the first one. It said to stop listening and write out a list of the things that needed to be done. "I was driving the car, so I quit listening and never got back to it."

He isn't watching his diet and knows he is doing nothing to help himself, but "I'm planning on getting to it." When told that he apparently doesn't consider himself worth the bother, he insists that isn't true. Then he laughs when I point out that his actions speak louder than his words. "I guess so," he says, but he makes no effort to change.

Some people neither seek nor value peace of mind. Like some radio and TV talk show hosts, they carry on in righteous indignation. They seem proud of their negative opinions, and come across as intentionally unhappy.

There are those too who won't find peace until they get honest with themselves. Examples include sneak-drinking members of Alcoholics Anonymous, Overeaters Anonymous members cheating on their food program, alcoholics abstaining from alcohol without a recovery program, and people in general who need, but refuse to join, any one of the Twelve Step recovery programs.

And, of course, there's that large group who agree that we should enjoy life—but not just yet! Their life has to be fixed before it can be enjoyed. They're the people who can see the problems but not the joy in life.

Sadly, many people have been unhappy for so long they can't see the possibility of change. Besides, changing to a new way of life is frightening.

While their present situation is uncomfortable and they complain about it, there's a sense of security in the familiar. Complaining is a way of life. They habitually pouted during childhood to make their parents feel guilty for the way they were being treated. The habit persists now in adult life—even though their parents are often long since dead.

For these and other reasons, many of us never change. Remember, the choice belongs to us. Only we can decide how important emotional independence and emotional sobriety are, and what we are willing to do to obtain and maintain them.

Fear, pouting, low self-esteem and the other problems mentioned are only a few of the many impediments to emotional independence, and emotional independence is the very foundation of emotional sobriety. However, none of these are absolute impediments, and achieving emotional independence is like the A.A. program in that, while it may not be easy, it is quite simple.

2. THE READER

Interpersonal relationships. Life's most exciting adventure is the journey into ourselves, the discovery of who we really are. The journey begins in infancy and continues throughout our lifetime. It begins when we first notice, consciously or unconsciously, the way people react or respond to us when we (for example) laugh or cry. How we come across to others is reflected back to us by the way they then come across to us. We begin to see ourselves as we are seen by others. People become our mirror.

This mirroring is one of the major benefits of an intimate relationship between two people. Both partners benefit. This back and forth interplay is interpersonal communication at its finest, and is well worth the time and effort required for its cultivation. It is also one of the main reasons sponsorship is so important—for both parties. Each learns progressively more about themselves as they see themselves reflected back by the other. Personally, I have at times found this process to be quite painful—but always beneficial.

However, a major problem arises all too commonly when a relationship is used as a manipulation. The more dominant partner convinces the less dominant to accept an inferior role. Thereafter, the dominant one sets the emotional tone and manipulates the other to act and feel as instructed. This arrangement can be found in couples ranging from teenagers to those married many years. It is a form of spousal abuse, and the abuser can be of either sex. Of course, it only happens to people willing to give up their emotional independence—and unwilling to reclaim it.

One sees the opposite of this behavior in Al-Anon members who maintain their emotional equilibrium in spite of whatever the alcoholics and various non-alcoholics in their life are doing or not doing. When an alcoholic eliminates the allergy problem by removing the alcohol, he or she then faces the same problem as the Al-Anon member, that of not allowing others to determine how they feel.

In order to maintain their sobriety, recovering alcoholics can not afford to let others control how they feel. Likewise, in order to maintain their sanity, Al-Anon members can not allow others to control their feelings. Indeed, release from emotional domination by anyone is a *major* Al-Anon goal.

Resentments result from emotional domination. People who stay upset over a relationship which broke up years earlier give control of their feelings to a person no longer in their life. They not only suffer the pain of the past; they now, of their own volition, allow the offending person to "make" them feel bad today. Such situations result in self pity, an emotion with absolutely no redeeming social value, but which obviously feels good, at least for a brief interval, or it wouldn't be so popular.

Emotional independence, on the other hand, feels even better and evolves from doing whatever we need to do to be comfortable within ourselves. Once again, we are reminded of the statement in *The*

Twelve Steps And Twelve Traditions[1], "It is a spiritual axiom that every time we are disturbed, no matter what the cause, there is something wrong *with us*." I take this to mean that we need to take our eyes off what the other person has done to us and look at what we have done to ourselves.

Regarding this question of emotional stability, Bill W., one of the co-founders of Alcoholics Anonymous had this to say:

> The Next Frontier. I think that many old-sters who have put our A.A. "booze cure" to severe but successful tests still find they often lack emotional sobriety. Perhaps they will be the spearhead for the next major development in A.A.—the development of much more real maturity and balance (which is to say, humility) in our relations with ourselves, with our fellows, and with God.[2]

I understand this quotation to mean Bill W. hoped old-timers, having found physical sobriety in A.A., would now become the spearhead to the new frontier of emotional sobriety.

I find myself writing this manuscript and talking to others about controlling feelings when I'm not always able to control my own. At times, not only can I not control my feelings, I can't control my thinking or my actions.

---

[1] *Twelve Steps And Twelve Traditions*, p. 90.
[2] *Language of the Heart: Bill W's Grapevine Writings*, (New York: The A.A. Grapevine, Inc., 1988), p.236.

One night, a manic depressive member of our group, who sporadically stops taking his lithium, came to the meeting looking for trouble and attention. He walked in carrying a blaring radio. When asked, he turned it down but walked up the steps to the stage and stood there facing the audience. A former group secretary asked him to come down. He refused and responded with foul language. Throughout the meeting, he ignored the speaker and sat on the top step fiddling with his radio and rooting through his backpack.

At the end of the meeting, he turned up the volume on the radio and, carrying it on his shoulder, marched through the crowd coming as close as possible to people trying to carry on conversations. Twice I reached toward the radio when he came dangerously close to the woman to whom I was talking. The first time, he threatened me, stating that he was going to fight me if I "touched (his) personal property again." The second time he began cursing using the F... word. Annoyed, I stupidly argued with him. By now he was in control of both my feelings and my actions.

Later during the night, I realized how impractical my reaction had been. Everyone in that room behaved better toward him than I had. They displayed more emotional independence, more emotional sobriety, more maturity. I, on the other hand, allowed a person whose actions I didn't like to control my emotional sobriety.

An attitude of total acceptance and peace of mind doesn't come naturally to me. I must remain diligently on guard to prevent my feelings, thoughts and actions from being controlled by people and circumstances. My serenity, like finely spun glass, is extremely fragile. My natural tendency is to find fault, see the defect, disapprove, then not accept what I see. I completely forget that acceptance does not imply approval.

Being right. As mentioned earlier, Max and I have been married since 1939. Early in our marriage, when we argued, we regularly came to the conclusion that we never should have gotten married in the first place. In spite of that, our marriage today is the best it has ever been. Furthermore, never before have I experienced such a sense of fulfillment, peace and joy in my daily life.

Getting along as well as we do now wouldn't be so surprising if we weren't such extreme opposites. From that standpoint alone, we really never should have married. I'm a vertical thinker and Max is a horizontal thinker. When working on a problem, I like to bring it to a focus. I ask questions that provide the information needed to narrow the problem down until, like a pyramid, it comes to a point. When that happens, I've reached a decision as to what needs to be done next and what approach to take.

Max doesn't do it that way. She never has enough information, always wants more, always has one more question. On a particular matter, I may need for her to answer simply yes or no. I can spend all day trying to figure out how to ask the question in such a way that she can only answer yes or no. It never works—she always comes up with another question. She's like the Rabbi who, when asked, "Why do you Jews always answer a question by asking a question?" responded with, "Why do you ask?"

Max likes to watch TV—one channel at a time. I use the clicker. That's what clickers were invented for. All channels watched at once may add up to something worth watching.

When I'm finished with something, I put it away so I'll know where it is when I need it again. Max prefers to hunt.

I want to do it now. Max likes doing it "later."

What's *really* strange about these differences is that neither of us is wrong! We're both right. We're just different. Quite different. But not wrong.

The concept of neither of us being wrong has been difficult to accept. If I'm right and someone dramatically differs from me, how can they not be wrong? How can we differ so markedly, yet both be right?

But we are, and I've had to accept that fact— over and over again. Once again, acceptance, as distinct from approval, is the answer. Formerly, when Max disagreed with me, I thought of her as stubborn and almost deliberately trying to upset me. Today, I interpret it as my problem, as a deficiency in my ability to communicate effectively.

My life consists of my relationships with people, places, things and situations, and my communications to and about those relationships. Thus, my life is essentially an on-going communication exercise—a continuous test of my communication skills. This is true for all of us—particularly when it comes to interpersonal relationships.

I wouldn't have so much trouble with interpersonal relationships if it weren't for my special talent. The Bible says if you don't use your talent, it will be taken away from you. As mentioned, I have this special ability to see the fault, the defect, the thing that is wrong with any person, place, thing or situation. I see right to the core of the problem. Not only can I see it, I need to tell you about it because I'm sure you want to know.

While speaking at Club Med on the island of Eleuthera a while back, my mouth became dry, and this affected my voice. A nice young lady walked out of the meeting to bring me a paper cup of water. I thanked her, then somewhat facetiously added, ". . . but why did you bring this in a cup with a pointed bottom? I can't set it down."

Father Tom talked the next day, and I noticed there was no place at the lectern to set his cup of coffee. He set it on the floor, and every time he wanted a drink, he had to bend down to get it. After he finished his talk, I mentioned to Owen, who records the meetings, that I was searching for a small stand or something to put beside the lectern to support the speaker's beverage. He said the Club Med staff had built the podium (the raised platform) and the lectern (the upright stand in front of the speaker) specifically for our use. He said he'd ask if they could add a little shelf to the side of the lectern.

By the very next meeting, a small shelf had been attached to the lectern—but on the left side! Upon seeing the shelf I had two simultaneous thoughts: That's really fast service getting that shelf up there so quickly, and why the devil did they put it on the wrong side? At every meeting thereafter I watched the speaker reach in front of themselves every time they wanted a drink.

I kept my peace, but thought to myself, if they ever decide to put that shelf where it belongs, they ought to knock off about a third of it; it's too wide. At the same time they might as well round off those two sharp corners.

This sort of perfectionistic thinking isn't conducive to ideal interpersonal relationships. Besides, it interferes with really hearing what the speaker is saying.

I believe. I have no way of proving it, but I choose to believe that God is never surprised. Whatever happens, God knew it was going to happen exactly as it did. My Higher Power never makes mistakes. I can't imagine God—not *my* God—sitting at a giant computer and suddenly exclaiming, "Oh my God, look what I just did! I hit the wrong key!"

I don't know why bad things happen to good people or why so much evil exists in the world. It certainly isn't because God is unloving, unmerciful or unjust. Perhaps Rabbi Kushner[3] has a point when he suggests that God may be all-loving but not *all-powerful*. Kushner raises the possibility that the laws of nature (established before the creation of man) take precedence. Earthquakes kill people indiscriminately without questioning their moral status.

I choose to believe that absolutely everything, every blade of grass, is exactly where it has been known through all eternity it would be at this moment. Each of us is precisely where it has always

---

[3] Harold S Kushner, *When Bad Things Happen to Good People*, (New York: Random House, 1987), Audio Cassette.

been known we would be, doing exactly what we are doing right now.

I'm not saying God predetermines everything. I'm saying He or She has known all along that things would turn out as they have. God is not surprised. God is all-knowing, not all-controlling. Man does have free will.

God doesn't recognize a past or a future. Everything happens in the present for God. When we mind-trip into the past or future, we travel alone. God doesn't go with us. Or, so I choose to believe.

I have also made the decision to believe that you and I and every one of us have been doing the best we could at every moment of every day of our lives up to and including this moment. If we could have done better, we would have done better.

That contradicts what I was taught while growing up. I was repeatedly told I could have done better if I had tried harder. I prefer to believe I would have tried harder if I could have tried harder. I believe that mentally and emotionally, I was doing the best I could at the time regardless of how it appeared to others.

Furthermore, if this is true for me, then it is true for you and for every one of us. All along, we did the best we could under the circumstances at that particular time.

I can't prove it's true, but I choose to believe people treat me the way I've taught them to treat me. This creates a big responsibility for me. It means that if I don't like the way someone is treating me, I can alter their behavior by first changing my own. I can have a positive influence on the situation. Since I have, by my behavior, taught them to treat me the way they are treating me, I can often, by changing my behavior, teach them to treat me differently.

If I want them to change, I must change first. It is a basic psychological teaching that if we want to change the way we *feel*, we must first change the way we *act*. As I said, if I want someone to change their behavior toward me, I must first change my behavior toward them.

It's like playing tennis with a better player. You grow tired of losing. You wish they'd lose once in a while. But your opponent won't change until you change. When you improve your game to the point where you win, your opponent will lose. You must take the action of improving your game. You must change first.

Better still, change your behavior in such a way that neither partner loses and both win. I've watched this happen many times. My involvement has been more with men than with women. Because of childhood experiences, or for whatever reason, the man in these situations becomes fearful when the woman displays anger or serious displeasure. To prevent further discomfort, he goes along with whatever she wants. But secretly he resents her.

He doesn't fight—he's too afraid to argue or to express his unhappiness. Instead, he waits. He knows exactly what to say and do to upset her. When the time comes, he does so. As she becomes angry and says nasty things to him, he knows how to respond to upset her further. The more angry and hostile she becomes, the more aggressive he can become, because he now sees himself as defending himself against her insanity. Finally she becomes physically abusive and turns to dishes, knives, books, lamps and other objects to use in her acts of violence.

Now he says to anyone willing to listen, "Let me tell you what she did! Can you believe anyone would act like that? Have you ever heard of such insanity?"

His focus is on her and her actions with not one speck of insight into his own behavior and how he provoked the situation and then manipulated it to this final ridiculous stage.

Neither partner enjoys this game, yet they play it over and over. Each "knows" the other is at fault. The situation is exactly the same when the roles are reversed, when the dominant, abusive, violent partner is the man, and the woman plays the passive/aggressive, manipulative role. In a number of these situations I've been able to convince the man that his partner treats him the way she does because he has taught her to treat him that way.

I repeatedly tell him that if he wants to feel differently, he has to act differently. He must change his behavior, not hers. I tell him if he changes drastically enough and long enough, she will very likely change. She may temporarily get worse before she gets better, but she will change.

I remind him that The Big Book says in two places, one of them in italics, that we have ceased fighting anything and anybody. We can't fight our partner and work a good recovery program at the same time. So, do *not* fight. Absolutely refuse to fight. Instead, insist on your right to "Call for a break." Set a time to talk later rather than now.

Try to lighten up. If at all possible, instill a little humor. Above all, keep your mouth shut and carefully *listen* to what your partner has to say. If he or she gets really upset and starts making outlandish and insulting statements, absolutely do not retaliate. Do not stoop to that level. Instead, consider taking notes or saying you would like to call either your sponsor or their sponsor, so an outsider can be brought into the conversation. If the situation continues to seriously deteriorate, the best outsider to call can sometimes be the police. They're professionals at calming situations down.

Most such altercations can be prevented if we remember to not become upset when our partner is upset. Don't join them. Don't ever allow both of you to be upset at the same time. Whoever gets upset first, it's their turn—always. By keeping your mouth shut, by staying calm, you set the stage for your partner to join you where you are, as opposed to you joining them where they are. Be like the woman who takes the phone calls coming in from people complaining about the Los Angeles freeways. She says she enjoys her job and is able to handle it because her father taught her long ago that there's no such thing as a one-sided argument. She insists that she and the other person can't be screaming at each other if she's not screaming back.

When either partner makes the initial, necessary changes, both partners end up loving themselves and each other more than before. Intimacy in a relationship develops as a result of working through problems. Handled in this manner, a problem truly becomes a win/win situation. Everybody wins.

It's the difference between control and influence. We give up trying to control our partner's behavior. Instead, we try to influence their behavior in a positive direction. We do this by exercising choices in the way we act and in the way we communicate with them.

A measure of one's communication skill is the result it produces. If you don't like the results you are getting when communicating with another person, there's a great deal you can do about it. We will return to this idea because of it's importance.

At an Al-Anon meeting, I heard someone say, "The more you try to control another person, the more you are under that person's control." If how you feel or what you do next depends on what the person you are trying to control does or does not do next, then you are under that person's control.

A common example of this is described in the Al-Anon pamphlet *Understanding Ourselves and Alcoholism*[4]. Referring to persons in close relationships with alcoholics, it says, "They see that the drinking is out of control and they try to control it. . . . These well-meaning people begin to count the number of drinks another person is having. They pour expensive liquor down drains, search the house for hidden bottles, listen for the sound of opening cans. All their thinking is directed at what the alcoholic is doing or not doing and how to get the drinker to stop drinking."

---

[4] *Understanding Ourselves and Alcoholism*, (Virginia Beach, VA: Al-Anon Family Group Headquarters, Inc.,1979), Al-Anon pamphlet P-48.

I didn't immediately give up trying to control when I got sober. Neither do most alcoholics. And when the person the alcoholic is trying to control is either another alcoholic or an Al-Anon member who has also not given up trying to control, the difficulty is more than doubled. Add to this, children growing up in an alcoholic family, children who themselves have learned the art of manipulation and control, and you have the setup for chaos. This situation desperately needs the communication skills involved in obtaining and maintaining emotional sobriety through emotional independence.

I also choose to believe that if I do a thing for the right motive and leave the results up to God, everything will turn out the way it is supposed to. Not necessarily the way I would have chosen, but definitely the way it is supposed to be.

I read somewhere that we forget most of what we read—especially the stuff in self-help books. I'm lucky if I sometimes remember the title. On the other hand, the title is often all I need. For example: *Feel Your Fear and Do It Anyway*, or *What You Think of Me Is None of My Business*. The titles remind me of the basic principle that I need to remember.

If we're both lucky, by the time you put this book down, you will be convinced that people and circumstances don't make us angry; *we* make ourselves angry. People *can't* make us angry—unless we let them. We alone are responsible for our feelings.

If you accept that single fact, and remember only the title of this book, you will have come a long way, a longer way than many people in our society, in maintaining your serenity and peace of mind.

If we alcoholics are to remain physically sober, we must remain emotionally free; free of the control of people who might otherwise "drive us to drink." This requires courage, more courage than many people have. Specifically, it requires the courage to change our thinking, our attitudes and our behavior in many small ways. It also requires skill, knowledge and practice, lots of practice. It also requires a willingness to reach out to others for their experience, strength and guidance.

Before sobriety, the practicing alcoholic turned his or her life over to the care of alcohol, while the alcoholic's partner often turned their life over to the alcoholic. Neither took a leadership role in their own life. In recovery, everyone, both alcoholic and non-alcoholic, with the help of God and a good recovery program, accepts a leadership role and finds emotional independence, the subject of the next chapter.

3. THE ANSWER

Emotional Independence. I've been writing and talking about the concept of emotional independence for quite some time now. Because I believe written agreements are more difficult to ignore than verbal contracts, and as I mentioned earlier, in 1990 I gave Max a written Declaration of Emotional Independence. It stated that she was no longer responsible for my feelings and I was no longer responsible for hers. My anger and all my feelings, I admitted, came from me, not from her. From that point on, I could no longer say, "You made me angry." I could only say, "I chose to get angry when you did what you did."

In addition, neither of us could ever again pout in an effort to make the other feel guilty for how we felt. Our feelings became our personal responsibility and could no longer be blamed on our partner.

It has indeed been a great freedom to no longer be responsible for anyone else's feelings. It has been an equally great freedom to not have my feelings controlled by anyone other than myself.

Without emotional independence, I can't have emotional sobriety. I can't be content unless every person, place, thing and situation in my life is precisely the way I want it to be—and stays that way. If I give away my emotional independence and allow any other person to control my emotions, then they control not only my emotional sobriety but possibly also my physical sobriety.

Recently I listened to Steve Chandler's audio tape *35 Ways to Create Great Relationships*[1]. I agree with everything he said about emotional independence which he listed as his most important item.

Even more important though, is the stress he places on our ability to *create* our relationships rather than to merely *react* to the various people and events that come into our lives. He points out that if we aren't *creators,* then we are habitual *reactors.* He says most people looking for help with relationship problems react all day to the actions of other people and thereby generate their own negative reactions to people. This, he insists, is a habit, and like any other habit, it can be changed. He quotes Ralph Waldo Emerson as having asked, "Why should my happiness depend on the thoughts going on in someone else's head?"

I'm so accustomed to letting others control my feelings and letting my feelings control my actions that I often forget that I have choices. I don't remember to stay self-centered—centered in myself. Once I allow someone else to dictate my emotional state, regaining control is impossible until I become aware of what I have done. I have voluntarily given up control. I have allowed someone else to choose how I am going to feel. Not until I am aware of what has happened, can I decide what I want to do about it. Awareness must come first.

---

[1] Steve Chandler, *35 Ways to Create Great Relationships,* (St Paul, MN: HighBridge Co., 1998), audio cassette.

I'm not willing to let any thing or any person put my physical sobriety at risk; why should I put less value on my emotional sobriety? Besides, I like the feeling I have when I conduct myself in an emotionally mature, independent manner.

Emotional maturity is like serenity. The first time I felt serene, I wondered what was happening, but I liked the feeling and wanted more. The more I got, the more I wanted. Serenity is addictive.

So is emotional independence. I get the same sort of good feeling when I think, speak and act assertively. On the other hand, I dislike myself when I act like a passive wimp or an aggressive bully. It feels good to feel good, and I want all the good feeling I can get.

Essentially, emotional maturity demands on-going, total acceptance of people, places, things and situations as they are, rather than as I might wish them to be. An A.A. friend says that each day, however things are in his life that day, he tries to love it, because that's the way it's going to be any-way. Being unhappy and disgruntled changes noth-ing but our mood—and that for the worse.

As mentioned earlier, the concept of acceptance is well-worded in *Courage to Change*[2], a book of daily readings, in the section for September 12th.

In dealing with a change, a problem, or
a discovery, awareness is often followed
by a period of acceptance before we can

---

[2] *Courage to Change*, (Virginia Beach, VA: Al-Anon Family Group Head-quarters, Inc.,1992), p. 256.

take action. This process is sometimes referred to as the "Three A's" — Awareness, Acceptance, and Action.

Coping with a new awareness can be extremely awkward, and most of us are eager to spare ourselves pain or discomfort. Yet, until we accept the reality with which we have been faced, we probably won't be capable of taking effective action with confidence.

Still, we may hesitate to accept an unpleasant reality because we feel that by accepting, we condone something that is intolerable. But this is not the case. As it says so eloquently in One Day at a Time in Al-Anon (ODAT), *Acceptance does not mean submission to a degrading situation. It means accepting the fact of a situation, then deciding what we will do about it. Acceptance can be empowering because it makes choice possible.*

For me the choice commonly centers around situations such as someone talking at me in what I consider to be an unnecessarily rude and hostile manner. My choices include assuming the role of follower and behaving as that person is behaving, or instead, assuming the role of leader and conducting myself in a manner of *my* choosing, that is, a manner superior to and independent of that person. Am I now going to mimic that person's bad attitude and make the situation worse, or am I going to be the person I want to be?

While writing this, the proper choice seems obvious. However, in practice I commonly make the wrong choice without giving it any thought. I don't ask myself how I want to emotionally handle the situation. Instead, I automatically think I need to defend myself, to stand up for myself, to not let anyone get the better of me, to not be passive and intimidated. In other words, to "win."

I forget that my greatest defense lies in my defenselessness. Being basically powerless, I have no defense. Having no defense, I choose to rise above the immediate situation rather than lower myself to that person's standard of behavior.

My tendency to fight comes from my insecurity, something we all feel at times, and which causes us to join others in their aggressive behavior. By feeling secure in my defenselessness, I am able to be my own person. I behave like a successful member of A.A., like a person who practices the Twelve Steps in all his affairs and has ceased fighting everything and everybody. I literally *win* by not taking the bait, by not fighting.

This, of course, brings up the question, do we never stand up for ourselves and for what is right? Are we doormats?

Definitely not. The difference, as I see it, is that we get on with our lives. We don't sit around letting that situation decide our emotional state. We don't get caught in the trap of letting the situation upset us and then having to stay upset waiting for the situation to change to our satisfaction.

Instead, we accept our powerlessness over the fact of the situation and then calmly do what we can to improve the situation. We trust in God's will knowing that, in general, we are far more efficient and effective when we respond calmly and in an unhurried manner than when we explode in unthinking anger.

Exploding can be a really bad trap. Having exploded, some of us are too proud to make amends, and are thus forced to spend a major part of our lives stewing in unhappy emotions.

Learning how.   All of this is easier to say than to do. Yesterday, while trying to balance the credit card account, I asked Max for the bills for the last three months. She told me to get them myself— "back there" in the storage room. I had no idea what she was talking about and I became angry and loud. She merely repeated what she had said and walked off into the bedroom. In a moment of fury, I picked up one of the dog's plastic toys and hurled it against the wall—distinctly *aggressive* behavior.

A short time later, while walking the dog, I realized that, earlier while cleaning out the storage room, I'd given Max a stack of photographs and papers and asked her to decide where she wanted me to put them.

I like things put away. Max likes things left where they are. More than anything, she hates having others put her things away for her. When I remembered this, I realized she wasn't upset because I had asked for the last three month's records. She was annoyed because I'd been straightening up her storage room. In her mind, I had probably thrown out many of her possessions including the records I now couldn't find. She hadn't complained when I asked for her help, but now she was probably thinking, "You didn't ask for my opinion when you were throwing those things away, don't ask for my help now."

After we quietly and *assertively* (neither *passively* nor *aggressively*) discussed what had happened, we felt closer to each other—as so often happens following a disagreement.

All that was required of me was to quietly ask Max if we could talk. When she agreed, I took the opportunity to tell her that I was concerned when she became upset earlier in the day when I asked for the old bills. "Did I do something in particular that upset you?" I asked.

Then I remained silent while she told me again how annoyed she gets when I disturb things that belong to her. "Those are my things, and I really wish you'd leave them alone," she said. After we both said everything we had to say, we agreed that our love for each other was more important than bills or other material things. At the end of the session, we both agreed that hereafter we would each make a special effort to treat the other with more courtesy and respect.

Couples feel comfortable together when they talk and act assertively, and they feel even more intimate after they've talked their way through a difficult situation. They also find out who they are as individuals by this process of working their way through problems.

There are a number of helpful books which give specific directions for accomplishing this. One is Harville Hendrix's *Getting The Love You Want, A*

Guide For Couples.[3] Hendrix believes we picked our current partner because of unfinished childhood needs associated with our parents. According to this idea, conflicts between you and your partner do not necessarily mean you were not meant for each other. Instead, it means you have chosen the person most able to help you grow in emotional maturity.

Hendrix tells couples precisely how to *assist* their partner while that partner works out their individual childhood-onset personality problems. This, of course, is in marked contrast to the usual habit of each telling the other what is wrong with them and what they ought to do about it. We will come back to Hendrix' methods a bit later.

Psychiatrist Tom Rusk no longer practices conventional psychotherapy. Instead, he prefers to reach more people by writing books and giving seminars to teach individuals how to achieve personal emotional growth on their own. In *The Power of Ethical Persuasion—Winning Through Understanding at Work and at Home,*[4] he tells people how to recognize and deal with their feelings, and how to help others do the same thing by working through their mutual communications problems. Like Hendrix, he places great emphasis on listening. He lists three phases of ethical persuasion: First, exploring the other's position (listening), then explaining your viewpoint, and finally creating resolution. His

---

[3] Harville Hendrix, *Getting The Love You Want, A Guide For Couples* , (New York: Henry Holt & Company, Inc. 1988), p. 249.

[4] Tom Rusk M.D., *The Power of Ethical Persuasion—Winning Through Understanding at Work and at Home*, (New York: Penguin Books USA Inc., 1994) p. 22.

method is similar but somewhat simpler than that of Hendrix.

On a less professional level, there's George Thompson's *Verbal Judo—The Gentle Art of Persuasion.*[5] I don't particularly care for the word Judo. It sounds war-like even though I know Judo to be a program of non-resistance. For example, Judo instructors insist that you not brace yourself to resist when an assailant comes charging at you. Instead, at the last moment, step to one side, take hold of your assailant and let his forward motion throw him to the ground.

Similarly, Thompson urges his readers to not allow the aggressive words and manner of an adversary to have their intended harmful effect. He takes obvious pleasure in defusing potentially explosive situations, often with levity and humor, and in teaching others how to do it themselves. He wants people to enjoy their ability to remain calm in difficult situations, and to see that, by doing this, they maintain control of both their personal emotional life and the situation itself.

Behaving in the manner Thompson describes is thoroughly enjoyable, but it certainly contrasts with my basic nature. I'm more like my little dog Sabrina. Sabrina can't stand having another dog bark within her earshot, and especially not at her directly. It drives her wild—even though she can't see them. She's completely blind, but if another dog barks

---

[5] George Thompson, *Verbal Judo—The Gentle Art of Persuasion*, (New York: Quill, William Morrow, 1993).

even while traveling in the opposite direction on the other side of the street, the hair goes up on the back of her neck and she bounces up and down while charging against her leash, barking, growling and trying to cross the street. As we continue to walk, she stays upset and continues to growl and complain. She tries to chase any motorcycle or truck that goes by making a strange noise, and for quite some time thereafter she looks around for anyone to fight with. All of this is, of course, way out of proportion to the imagined danger. In fact, there was no danger in the first place.

I'm like that if I'm not careful. Especially the part about continuing to ruminate about how I could have handled the situation better, long after the offending person is no longer around. Now, with practice, I realize increasingly more often how much more important my emotional sobriety is than that person or that situation, and I don't allow what happened to ruin the rest of my day. As mentioned before, it feels good to be emotionally independent and in control of both myself and what would otherwise be an uncomfortable situation.

As suggested by many authors, *listening* to one's adversary is extremely important, but I often find it difficult to keep my mouth shut in the heat of the situation. One method that has helped in this regard is for me to ask relevant questions. What do you mean when you say that? How long have you felt that way? What is it that you want? Just what would you like me to do? Or any similar question seeking basic information.

Such questions not only clarify the problem, they evoke a sense of emotional stability and of directly participating in the discussion. If nothing else, when it works I'm at least listening to answers to my own questions.

In *Why Marriages Succeed or Fail . . . And How You Can Make Yours Last*,[6] John Gottman makes a most interesting and extremely critical distinction between *complaining* and *criticizing*. He stresses the wisdom of complaining, of expressing rather than storing negative feelings. These feelings belong to you, not the other person. Expressing them is a proper way of handling them. But criticizing, on the other hand, constitutes a direct attack on your partner's character.

Gottman points out the ease with which we unwittingly cross the line between complaining and criticizing. To distinguish between the two, he points out that complaints often begin with "I," and criticisms begin with "You." Notice the contrast between "I'm bothered by this clutter." (a feeling and an honest and not particularly hurtful statement), and "You're a terrible housekeeper" (an opinion and a direct attack). Similarly, "I don't care for that dress" is not the same as "You look fat!" A further example would be when you complain to your partner about being spoken to in an unnecessarily rude tone of voice and are told, "Oh, Poor Baby! You're just too sensitive!"

Be particularly careful when you offer a complaint about your partner's sexual behavior. This is often heard as a personal criticism rather than a

---

[6] John Gottman, *Why Marriages Succeed or Fail . . . And How You Can Make Yours Last,* (New York: Fireside, 1994,) p. 234.

complaint. Indeed, some partners are so insecure that they never hear any complaint as anything other than a criticism of their character, in which case they then respond with character assassinations.

A great many relationships have been destroyed or seriously impoverished by lack of awareness of this extremely important distinction between complaints and criticisms. Actually, it's a matter of adhering to that portion of the Twelfth Tradition which reminds us to *keep principles before personalities.*[7] We adhere to the principle of honestly stating our feelings, but we do not discuss personalities.

In *How to Argue and Win Every Time*[8], Gerry Spence repeatedly points out the foolishness of being fearful in a communication situation since our opponent has only as much power and influence over us as we choose to give him or her. What Spence says is unquestionably true. However, many of us, in spite of respectable lengths of time in recovery, still all too frequently lose our serenity over simple, everyday encounters.

We focused on this problem of getting upset over trivialities one night in a small, informal men's meeting. The list of people and things that at times upset us went on and on. It included spouses, adolescent and older children, employers, employees, patients, clients and customers, relatives and neighbors, and other drivers on the freeway. It often took

---

[7] *Alcoholics Anonymous*, p. 564.

[8] Gerry Spence, *How to Argue And Win Every Time*, (New York: St. Martin's Press, 1995).

very little to seriously disturb some of us. Although we frequently asked God to grant us serenity via the Serenity Prayer, we abruptly, for frivolous reasons, threw away whatever serenity we had. Being a group of reasonably intelligent men, I wondered why this would be so.

Apparently this odd behavior reflects the different value each person, at different times, puts on his emotional sobriety. For many of us, emotional sobriety fluctuates wildly in personal value.

Besides, it's frightening to change; so frightening that Webster has a word for it. "*misoneism* (mis-uh-NEE-izm), the hatred or fear of change or innovation."

Routinely we ask God via the Serenity Prayer for the courage to change, then fail to act courageously; we don't change. While complaining about a situation, we enjoy the sense of security that accompanies the familiar. Suppose we changed, and things were no better—or maybe even worse. Who would we blame then?

This business of blaming is important. When we're upset, as long as we can blame our emotional state on a situation or another person, we have a sense of power, a sense of control over the alleged cause of our problem. Having appointed ourselves judge, jury and executioner, and having declared someone else "wrong," we feel superior to that person. Our thinking says such things as, "You can't treat me like that! I'm not going to let you get away with this! You'll be sorry!"

The more angry and abusive we become, the more powerful we feel. The more we lose control of our emotions, the more we try to control others. Deep down we may suspect the foolishness of our position, but if we stop fighting, we'll have to give up this feeling of power. Also, the other person will have "won."

Ultimately, we have no choice. For physical sobriety, we had to give up drinking, and for emotional sobriety, we have to give up blaming others. Totally. No longer can we say, "You made me angry!" Instead, we must accept personal responsibility for our emotional state. Every time we are upset, we must admit to ourselves that we have chosen to be upset, no one has *made* us upset.

This much responsibility may seem extreme, yet in fact it is a great freedom. Henceforth, no person or situation can upset us if we don't give them or it permission to do so. What in sobriety could be a greater freedom than that?

Brian Tracy[9] carries this idea even further. He says there are a total of 54 negative emotions such as fear, anger, depression, resentment, loneliness, etc., and he claims that every one of them is based on blame. Furthermore, he insists that anyone can eliminate all 54 negative emotions from their lives by accepting full responsibility for their feelings and thereby no longer blaming any other person or situation for how they feel.

When I started to follow Tracy's suggestion, this question of total responsibility became even worse. I discovered that I also had to accept respon-

---

[9] Brian Tracy, *The Psychology of Achievement*, (Chicago: Nightingale-Conant,) Audio Cassette.

sibility for my actions—actions which had resulted from highly-charged emotions which I had been blaming on others. This was brought to my attention by the February 20th page in Al-Anon's *Courage to Change* which states, "One of the first things I heard in Al-Anon was that we didn't have to accept unacceptable behavior. . . . A few years later, I was congratulating myself on how I no longer had such problems, when I suddenly realized there was still one person from whom I regularly accepted unacceptable behavior—me!"

In order to stop displaying the type of behavior that all too often erupted when people and circumstances upset me, I had to accept responsibility for both my emotions and my resultant actions. I had to stop putting the blame out there, and start looking in here at myself. Simply put, I had to start acting like a winner instead of a whiner.

The basic process, while not necessarily easy, is quite simple. Indeed, "Keep It Simple," is a primary A.A. motto. We'll come back to this idea in chapter 9, but, for now, people who know about such things insist there are only two basic emotions: Love and Fear. All other emotions, they say, are variations on either of these two themes. At every moment of every day we choose either love or fear.

While at first blush it may not seem *macho* to approach life from the standpoint of love, love is certainly more manly than fear.

Today, I have a choice. Before blowing up, or as quickly as possible thereafter, I can ask myself, am I reacting in fear or in love? I can modify the Serenity Prayer by saying, God, grant me either the ability to change this situation or the ability to change my attitude toward it.

Attitudes are contagious. When I chose a love-based life, I set the tone in my home and work place. Sadly, the same thing happens when I choose fear. We really do, I have found, get back what we put out.

Fear isn't the only emotion that causes us to give up our emotional independence. The sex urge, anger, resentment, embarrassment, intimidation, frustration, depression, illness, fatigue, hopelessness, guilt, confusion, anxiety, apprehension, antagonism, contempt, nervousness, apathy, inadequacy, disappointment, envy, anticipation—all these and many more rob us of our emotional independence and cause us to feel other than the way we wish to feel. To correct this situation, we must first become *aware* of how we feel. Then we must remember that we *can* change the feeling if we choose to. We don't have that choice until we realize that we have given our emotional independence away. Only then are we able to do something about it.

An enormous number of books, lectures, courses, seminars, audio and video tapes devoted to interpersonal communication skills are available in libraries and bookstores. Some teach how to "win" by being more aggressive and hostile than our opponent.

As aspiring "winners" in recovery, we are not interested in defeating anyone. Or even in fighting. *We have ceased fighting anything or anyone.*[10] Our

---

[10] *Alcoholics Anonymous*, p. 84.

interest lies in creating harmonious interpersonal relationships, in making potentially distressing situations better and in being peacemakers. We are interested in learning techniques whereby we assume a leadership role and demonstrate our emotional independence by our calm behavior.

We, not others, determine our attitude, our emotional state. We practice the principle mentioned earlier: *Acceptance does not mean submission to a degrading situation. It means accepting the fact of a situation, then deciding what we will do about it.* We carry the message of recovery by conducting ourselves as successful members of our respective recovery programs. To accomplish this, we practice and develop skill in interpersonal communications.

4. THE BASICS

Communicating. Life consists of one communication situation after another. If we don't communicate effectively, we don't succeed in life generally or in relationships in particular. In my previous book, *There's More to Quitting Drinking Than Quitting Drinking*, I discussed several different aspects of recovery including physical, mental, emotional, marital, and spiritual sobriety. I also addressed problems related to the use of prescription drugs and the question of sleeping without benefit of pills. Now in this current book, the emphasis is on maintaining emotional sobriety and peace of mind whether or not one is an alcoholic (or otherwise chemically addicted), and regardless of whatever else is going on in one's life.

The trick to accomplishing this monumental feat includes not only a good Twelve Step spiritual recovery program, but also skill in dealing with emotions (yours and someone else's) and in communicating effectively on an interpersonal level.

Some of the information needed to acquire this skill was covered in my earlier book, but because of its relevance to what we are talking about now, I will summarize it here.

Concerning feelings, the most important point to remember is that everyone has them, and we should never be ashamed nor apologize for feeling the way we do. Feelings have no moral value. They may be pleasant or unpleasant, but they are never morally good or bad. Only actions have moral value.

Feelings are best handled by expressing them, and worst handled by denying them, by pretending they don't exist.

As for interpersonal communication skill, no single factor is more important than learning to communicate assertively (as distinct from communicating passively or aggressively). Assertiveness is *not* a mild form of aggressiveness. In aggressive communications, the other person is hurt by the manner in which you express your feelings. In passive communications, you accept the hurt yourself rather than take what appears to be a risk of hurting the other person by telling them truthfully how you feel.

Let me stress that the words are "how you feel," not "what you think." The difference can be monumental. For example, "You are disgusting." versus "I am embarrassed."

In assertive communications, you express your feelings (not opinions) honestly and sincerely in such a way that no one gets hurt. You end up feeling good about yourself and your honesty.

Saying, "I feel . . . [happy, sad, glad, angry, upset, (whatever)]" expresses a *feeling*. Saying, "I feel that . . . ." expresses an *opinion*. Adding "that" to the sentence changes it completely. Failure to recognize this difference leads to misunderstandings and arguments. We are often called upon to defend our opinions; we need never defend our feelings.

In *That's Not What I Meant*[1], Deborah Tannen explains how parents teach their children to talk. Without thinking about it, they teach a conversational style. It's their own natural style, and there's nothing essentially wrong with it. But later in life it can be significantly different from the style of one's partner.

Furthermore, in spite of the importance of this difference, it may not be apparent to either the participants or to a casual observer. The participants are more likely to think of themselves as intelligent people who simply need to talk their problems out. However, when their different conversational styles cause irritation and confusion, the more they talk, the worse the problem becomes. Outside help may be required.

Early in sobriety Max and I read John Powell's *Why Am I Afraid To Tell You Who I Am?*[2] Powell taught us the value of distinguishing different levels of interpersonal communications. We now think in terms of five levels:

1. Cocktail Chit-Chat

    The most superficial level.

    Important because conversations start

    here and move up.

    "How are you?"

    "Fine."

    "Nice day."

    "What's up?"

---

[1] Deborah Tannen, *That's Not What I Meant* (New York: Ballantine Books, 1986).

[2] John Powell, *Why Am I Afraid To Tell You Who I Am?*, (Niles, IL: Argus Communications, 1969).

2. Talking About Others
"Have you seen Charlie?"
"How's that fellow you were spon-
soring?"
"Did you know Jack was celebrating
his birthday on Saturday?"

3. Expressing Ideas, Judgments, Opinions
"I like the format of this meeting."
"I liked what the speaker said about
sponsorship."
"People are sure friendly here."

4. Expressing Feelings, Emotions, Attitudes
"I had the most delightful experience
today."
"I'm depressed."
"I need to talk to you about a resent-
ment."

5. Peak Communications
Extreme closeness. The ultimate in
intimacy. Those periods of flawless
harmony when both are fully aware
that their reactions and emotions are
shared completely and perfectly by
their partner. For example, those occasional, brief periods of complete
and perfect communication between
close friends or sex partners.

Max and I know a couple whose marriage counselor told them, "Your marriage isn't working. I
recommend a divorce." They left his office in silence. After lunch the husband said, "I don't know
what you're going to do, but I'm going to that

couple's communications workshop. You can come along if you want."

A year later at the same workshop and still married, they couldn't find the words to express their joy. They discovered that nothing was wrong with their relationship which couldn't be overcome by learning to communicate effectively.

Incidents of this type, plus our own personal experience, convinced Max and me that if we wanted a happy and successful relationship, we would have to develop our interpersonal communication skills. We seemed to need more help in this area than just about anyone we knew. We needed it then, and we continue to need all the help we can get in communicating effectively now.

In our search for help, we came across the work of two marriage counselors, David and Vera Mace, who practiced their profession together for fifty years. During the first twenty-five years, they worked with couples in trouble, couples breaking up because of problems such as money, sex, in-laws and children. During the second twenty-five years they founded what they called Marriage Enrichment, an organization devoted to the improvement of good marriages. They discovered that these marriages survived the same problems (money, sex, in-laws, children) that allegedly created the havoc in troubled relationships.

After years of study, the Mace's came to the conclusion that healthy marriages had three distinct features that were lacking in troubled marriages. Essentially, these were:

1. *A commitment to the spiritual and emotional growth of one's partner;*
2. *A commitment to learn and to practice communication skills;*
3. *A commitment to resolving conflicts creatively.*

When I first read this, I thought, What an order! But then I began to see the similarities to the A.A. and Al-Anon programs. When both partners in a relationship go to one or both programs and encourage the rest of the family to do the same, they demonstrate their commitment to each other's emotional and spiritual growth.

As for learning communication skills, where would A.A. and Al-Anon be without communications, without the caring and honest sharing that activate the meetings? And where better to practice these skills than at home?

The third item, creative problem solving, becomes a necessity when, as mentioned earlier and as stated in The Big Book of Alcoholics Anonymous, *We have ceased fighting anything or anyone.* It is impossible for two people to live in essentially the same space without generating conflicts, and when fighting is no longer an option, we are forced to find alternatives. We stop our old behavior, and experiment with new approaches.

Not fighting doesn't mean the "silent treatment." It means dealing with conflicts in a non-adversarial way without reacting either defensively or offensively. Each time Max and I give up one of these high-energy techniques that don't work and funnel our energy into a more effective approach, we find the changed behavior less difficult than anticipated.

What could be better in sobriety than two people living together and committing themselves on a daily basis to their partner's spiritual and emotional growth, learning and practicing communication skills, solving conflicts creatively and building their partner's self esteem by assuring them of their importance?

A measure of the effectiveness of communication is the result it produces. In other words, if you don't like what happens when you communicate with your partner or someone else, change your actions, change what you are doing. I have found that the more I change my behavior—the way I communicate—the more other people and situations change.

You can prove this for yourself by trying it, but you may have to try more than one approach before you see the benefit. We'll outline a variety of different approaches in later chapters.

Communicating in a relationship. Interpersonal relationships consist of two multifaceted personalities exposing to each other different aspects of themselves while they continually change as they grow in recovery. Such a complex dance cannot proceed without communication. When two people are together, there is no such thing as "no communication." Refusing to speak is communication. The sex act is communication.

Every relationship is an on-going exercise in communication skill. Indeed, life consists of relationships (among people, places, things, situations and combinations thereof), and of communications with and about those relationships. As such, life is a continuous communication problem.

Here's a relationship quiz: You and your partner have not been getting along well lately. Suddenly you are accused in a loud and angry voice of something you didn't do. Do you react, or do you respond?

Professional counselors make an important distinction between these two activities. The first implies an immediate answer; the second connotes thoughtful consideration before replying. The knee-jerk reaction of practicing alcoholics when confronted with a problem is to immediately become angry and drink. In recovery, although alcoholics give up drinking, they don't always give up reacting instantly in an unthinking and destructive manner.

1. Reacting

Here are a few of the reactions some of us have tried:

Completely forget the Steps, Slogans, Big Book and recovery.
Instead, focus exclusively on the problem.
Mirror the other person's abusive behavior.
Insist they are making us act the way we are acting.
Insist on controlling the other person's behavior and mood.

Of course, this puts us completely under that person's control. What we do next depends entirely on whether or not they do what we want them to do.

Continue to punish the other person even when we want to make up.

They haven't suffered enough yet. Don't tell them what's wrong, or what we want, or what we are thinking. If they loved us, they'd know. They'd be able to read our minds, the same way we read theirs.

Develop a long list of "should's" and "ought's."

"I should...; she should...; we ought..."

Obsess on, "If only...," and "What if...."

"If only I hadn't said that." "What would have happened if...?

Demand to know "Why?"

Refuse to be consoled until someone explains to our complete satisfaction why reality is the way it is.

Fight.

Do this either overtly (aggressively) or covertly (passive/aggressively).

Pout.

"I feel miserable, and everyone else should feel miserable too!"

Escape into health.

"I'm just fine. You're the one that's crazy."

Get angry.
> Kick the dog. Yell at the kids. Punish. Become defiant. Run away. Sleep somewhere else. Refuse to talk.

Play the martyr.
> Assume a passive role. Submit. Acquiesce. Comply. Be the victim. Have an anxiety attack.

Plan your suicide.
> "I'll show you; I'll kill me!"

We could increase the list *ad infinitum.*

* * *

A number of professionals have suggested names for some of the negative ways of reacting in a communication situation. Here are examples.

Self Justifying.
> This is extremely common in relationships and results from a desire to "win." It consists of each person hearing the voice and the words but not the message of the other, and then restating what they, themselves (rather than their partner), have already said. It sounds like this:
> He, "Yackety, yackety, yackety."
> She, "Chatter, chatter, chatter."
> He, "What I said was, 'Yackety, yackety, yackety.'"
> She, "And what I said was, 'Chatter, chatter, chatter.'"

He, "But can't you see that I'm saying,
'Yackety, yackety, yackety?'"

She, "So!! Well, why won't you admit
that I'm saying, 'Chatter, chatter, chatter?'"

He, "How can you be so damn stupid?"

She, "My Gawd! *You're* the one
that's *Stupid!*"

Defensiveness.

This occurs when we "know" we are
right and feel the need to explain our
position again and again. It causes a
great deal of needless difficulty between
couples. Since we've admitted in recovery that our lives have become unmanageable, our best defense (as stated earlier) is often our defenselessness. In Al-
Anon we hear, "Don't complain and
don't explain." Especially don't ever
explain your feelings. You feel the way
you feel because that's the way you
feel. No one said feelings have to be
logical, and you don't need anyone's
permission to feel them.

Talking Over.

This is starting to talk before the other
has finished speaking. Many families,
especially in certain cultures, talk this
way all the time. It's their style, their
manner of carrying on a conversation.
Under these circumstances there's nothing wrong with it. But to an uninitiated,
unsuspecting partner in a relationship

not raised to communicate in this manner, it can be confusing, intimidating and infuriating. In addition, the cause of the problem may not be apparent to either partner.

"Yeah-butting."

This often precedes Talking Over and is commonly heard at meetings when the newcomer responds to everything said with, "Yeah, but...".

Mind Reading.

The equivalent of, "Yes, that's what you said, but I know what you meant."

Cross-complaining.

This is a form of defensiveness. When your partner complains about you, complain about her. Anytime she mentions anything she doesn't like about you, tell her things you don't like about her. This snowballs and results in a non-conversation or worse.

Kitchen Sinking.

Cross-complaining at its best. Throw in every rotten thing you can think of except the kitchen sink.

Catastrophizing.

This involves gross exaggeration of the absolutely horrendous, insurmountable, catastrophic outcome if things don't turn out the way you think they should.

I Win, You Lose.

This is when we make winning more important than being loving; or wanting the other to lose even if we, ourselves can't win. Since our partner is not our enemy and the problem is only a challenge, we should stick to being loving. That way we both win, both grow, and nobody loses.

Getting Off The Beam.

Here you both lose sight of what the conversation was about. Everything said makes the situation worse and a fight is developing. Stop talking. Agree to "draw a line" and start over from a new base without repeating anything already said. Teamwork of this sort solves problems.

Rudeness.

This comes from treating your wife like "a wife," or your husband like "a husband." Instead, treat your mate like a secret lover. We have different styles of speaking in different relationships and under different circumstances. Ask yourself if your current style is appropriate and is it getting you what you want.

2. Responding

Okay, so you didn't react. You took time to get with yourself, to get centered in yourself, to maybe even suggest, "Let's talk about this." By not reacting, by simply avoiding the impediments to effective communication, your conversational skills will improve—and hopefully your partner's will begin to improve also.

Now, to further improve the situation, you might respond with empathy. All good listeners practice empathy.

When your partner expresses emotions, thoughts or feelings, no matter how bizarre, do your best to understand and possibly even to share those emotions, thoughts or feelings. Empathy is the ability to say to one's self, "If I were this person in precisely this same situation, I'd feel exactly as he or she does."

To actually feel another's feelings to the point of suffering along with them is sympathy. Sympathy is what the pre-Al-Anon, "codependent" mother or father feels when their alcoholic gets into trouble, and they suffer as much as, or more than, the alcoholic does. Sympathy is exhausting; it leads to so-called "burnout." Empathy is energizing; it leads to harmony.

Here are a few ways to show your partner that you empathize with his or her feelings and opinions.

Validation involves convincing your partner that you are able to see things from their perspective and through their eyes. That is, if you had been born of their parents in their place and had all their life experiences, thoughts and assumptions, then you too would think and feel exactly the way they do.

Validation is an extremely important aspect of good communication. You are not saying you agree with them. You are saying you understand where their feelings and opinions may be coming from even though you don't necessarily share them. It's a matter of walking in the other person's moccasins for a moment, and the best way to demonstrate this is by active listening and then giving feedback.

Active Listening. This is an excellent technique for preventing resentments. After listening carefully, and before continuing, respond by asking, "What I heard you say was _____. Is that accurate?" You'll be surprised how often what you heard is not what your partner meant. The misunderstanding becomes apparent when you paraphrase.

Give Feedback by Paraphrasing. This involves repeating in your own words what you thought you heard your partner say. Clarifying meanings at this point eliminates a great deal of argument later. Someone once gave me a desk sign that read, "I know you believe you understand what you think I said, but I'm not sure you realize that what you heard is not what I meant."

In paraphrasing, be sure to cover two aspects of what you think you heard your partner say. Include both the facts (description of the incident as they saw it) and the feelings (how they apparently felt about it).

Of the two, feelings are the more important. However, they may have been expressed only non-verbally in such things as speed, volume or tone of voice, choice of words or facial expression. In other words, your partner may not actually tell you how they feel. It's up to you to make an assumption from the way they act. Indeed, at times the words may say one thing, but the apparent mood says something different. For example, "You say you aren't angry, but you sound resentful."

Remember, you don't have to agree with what was said. You merely say in your own words what you think you heard, and how you think he or she feels about it. If your partner disagrees with your interpretation, do not argue. Calmly ask for a clarification. Do not express your own opinions or feelings at this time, and do not ask them to defend what they said or how they felt.

For example, after hearing your partner describe a particularly trying day, you might say, "It sounds like you've had a bad day."

As in a game of charades, the key words are,
"Sounds like. . . ."
"Sounds like you're angry."
"Sounds like you're depressed."
"Sounds like. . . (whatever emotion is evident)."

Professional listeners use this technique when a client becomes angry at them. Since fighting with a client isn't practical, they say something like, "Thank you for that information. I'll process it later." An Al-Anon lady I know tells her husband, "Thank you for loving me enough to tell me how you feel," when he tells her he is angry with her. These are examples of validation by means of paraphrased feedback.

A Communication Formula. There's a world of difference between saying, "You made me angry," and, "I am angry." The first is an accusation. It claims that the other person is responsible for the way you feel. That's not possible. No one can make anyone else feel any particular emotion. We don't have that much power over each other.

Caring about another's feelings without feeling responsible for them makes for more pleasant and better communications. Even more satisfying is the ability to express one's own feelings without having to defend them.

Here's a formula for doing this:

- "I feel _____" (state how you FEEL, not what you THINK)

- "when you (do what you did) _____" (don't be judgmental or sarcastic)

- "in (such and such a situation) _____" (give a precise time and place)

For example:

"I feel embarrassed, put-down and unimportant when you talk over what I am saying, and change the subject before I have finished speaking like you did when we were with Bill and Jean last night."

When the other person's behavior has a direct effect on your life, you can include that fact. Here's how George expressed himself to his spouse:

"I feel frustrated and angry when you ignore our budget and go on a spree like you did yesterday, buying clothes and stuff we agreed not to buy. Now I can't pay this month's bills."

The formula becomes:

- "I feel _____ when you _(describe the action)_ because _____ "

In the beginning, you might try writing the statement out in order to say it correctly. After reading or stating it, do not argue. You have not made an accusation. Nothing needs to be defended. Remember, you have the right to have feelings and to express them. Indeed, in a relationship, expressing your feelings amounts to an "obligation" as well as a "right."

Many relationships break up because of failure of one of the partners in this regard. Remember the movie *Ordinary People* starring Mary Tyler Moore? The story was that of an ideal family which finally broke up because the wife and mother failed to honestly express how she felt.

The importance of expressing feelings was pointed out again just recently. In a conversation with a middle-aged couple about their new-found relationship and how wonderful it was, the woman said, "I've learned more about him in this past month than I learned about my first husband in all the years I was married to him."

* * *

So far, we've stressed the speaking aspect of interpersonal communication. We shouldn't neglect silence—intentionally not speaking. Silence plays an extremely important role in verbal communication. Depending on how it is used, it can be either golden or highly destructive. The "Silent Treatment"—refusing to communicate—can be deadly to a relationship. So can unnecessarily long, seemingly judgmental pauses after your partner has taken the risk of telling you something of serious concern to them.

On the other hand, it's a nice compliment to the person you are talking to, when you habitually pause for 3 to 5 seconds before responding to whatever they have said. It conveys the impression that you are interested and are giving thoughtful consideration to their words.

Compare that slight pause to the chatterbox who loves the sound of his or her own voice, and can hardly wait for you to take a breath so they can start talking again. What they have to say is far more important to them than anything you might have to say.

On the other hand, silence it isn't something to always be avoided. In a conversation, one person talks, then the other talks, and sometimes nobody talks. That's okay. It isn't necessary to compulsively fill the silences. Lovers in particular find this to be true. In this situation, silence can be a form of intimacy. Nervous individuals, on the other hand, become anxious and feel obliged to always think of something to say. They often chatter foolishly and say things better left unsaid.

Isn't it interesting that the same letters spell both "silent" and listen?"

5. MOTIVATION

Victimhood. This book isn't meant for everyone, and certainly not for chronic victims. Some people just aren't happy unless they're upset about something or somebody. Ask and they'll gladly tell you who or what is upsetting them.

Look at the people you know in unhappy relationships who do nothing but complain. They threaten to leave but don't. Or they don't stay away if they leave. Everything is their partner's fault. Their life's work is to keep the focus on their partner's defects. To appear happy would confuse the issue. Their partner might assume their behavior didn't matter; then they'd never change. Their only hope for happiness is to remain obviously unhappy until their partner sees what he or she is doing wrong, feels guilty and shapes up.

Even worse, this attitude often permeates both partners in the relationship. Each feels the same about the other. Each resents the way the other treats them. Each feels justified and self-righteous in their evaluation of the situation.

The truth may appear obvious to an outsider, but not to them. A localized, undeclared, covert civil war drags on. A war in which no one wins—certainly not children unlucky enough to be trapped in the relationship.

I've seen this situation often. And I've never had a partner agree with me when I tell them, "I hear you saying it's your partner's fault that you are unhappy, and you want them to change." They never agree. They deny the obvious. They prefer to remain the resentful victim of a "bad relationship."

Nothing is more destructive of emotional independence, and nothing is a greater impediment to a leadership role in one's emotional life than being victimized by resentments. By definition, such a person's life is a reflection of the behavior of others—others in the past, the present or the future.

As children, victims learned to pout and feel sorry for themselves. It felt so good they never gave it up. They haven't learned to live without it. As adults, they'd rather feel miserable and blame others than accept responsibility for their emotional life. If they did accept this responsibility and still felt as bad, or—heaven forbid—even worse, they'd have no one to blame but themselves. Chronic victims aren't up to that challenge, and their resentments are their excuse for staying emotionally where they are.

Victimhood, blaming others for our lives, must be a defect of character. Like an addiction, it certainly alters one's personality. Many never recover from it, and many alcoholics can't stay sober because of it.

Mabel W., for example, told the world by her actions, I'd rather be dead than go to Al-Anon and accept responsibility for my life! Before swallowing a bottle of sleeping pills, she took one final jab at her boyfriend by writing, "Now look what you've gone and made me do!" She died—one more example of "I'll show you, I'll kill me."

Mable and her friend had spent the afternoon sharing with Max and me what we thought were the joys of recovery. Apparently she didn't like what she heard. At any rate, she enjoyed her resentments and the victim role too much to give them up. She lacked the courage to change.

Victims of resentments. Victimhood gets its power from resentments, a word I rarely used before getting into recovery. *The Synonym Finder*[1] lists the following synonyms for resentment: indignation, offense, umbrage, righteous anger, disgust, wrath, fury, rage, displeasure, disapproval, dissatisfaction, unhappiness, annoyance, exasperation, aggravation, bitterness, malice, animosity, hatred, ill feelings, and ill will.

Listings under resent include: be offended at, feel displeasure at, be irritated by, be annoyed at, be indignant at, dislike, view with dissatisfaction, disagree with, harbor a grudge against, never forget or forgive, harbor revenge. One could add: angry at, ticked off at, mad at, irritated by, really dislike, can't stand, hate, feel cheated by, would like to kill, and on and on.

No matter what label we give the feeling, we have willingly put ourselves in the victim role, and have given the person or situation that wronged us control over our feelings, our serenity, our emotional sobriety, and, if we are alcoholic, possibly even our physical sobriety. The seeming pleasure of holding a resentment isn't worth all that.

Resentments contain a great deal of energy—enough to lead to war, murder and suicide. During my early years in private practice, I diagnosed alcoholism in a young woman and referred her to

---

[1] J. I. Rodale, *The Synonym Finder,* Revised, (Emmaus, PA: Rodale Press, 1978).

Alcoholics Anonymous. Her husband happened to be the most powerfully built man I personally have ever known. He bragged about how, if a man standing at the bar expressed negative feelings about someone at the other end of the bar, he would walk down there and break the man's arm just to do the first man a favor.

When his wife decided to get sober, he insisted anybody could do that. To prove his point, he announced that he would join A.A. and quit drinking just long enough to take a one-year anniversary cake. And that's what he did.

After his one-year anniversary, he returned to the bar. He roughed up a man standing there. The man developed a resentment and went home. He loaded a shotgun and returned to the bar. He unloaded the shotgun into the strong man. The blast blew the strong man into eternity as quickly as if he had been quite puny. And it blew the man with the resentment into the penitentiary. Resentments are indeed powerful.

In *The Sermon On The Mount*[2], Emmet Fox wrote the best non-program method I have found for getting rid of resentments.

Fox insists that, as long as we harbor a resentment toward any other person, we should **not** say the Lord's Prayer. We should not ask God to, "Forgive us our trespasses as we forgive those who trespass against us," because, by doing so, we ask God to feel toward us and to treat us the way we feel toward and treat those we resent.

---

[2] Emmet Fox, *The Sermon On The Mount*, (San Francisco: Harper San Francisco, 1989), pp. 168-176.

Fox discusses at length the absolute necessity of forgiveness in pursuing a spiritual way of life. He talks about the total destructiveness of resentments and the way in which they spiritually chain us to the person we dislike. Finally, he describes the actual process of forgiveness.

This, he says, is not a thing to be done casually. Pray and get ready for it. When you are ready, get by yourself, pray for guidance, and finally give the entire matter and everything conncected to it to God.

Tell God you are giving this person and the entire business to Him, complete in *every* detail. From this moment on, it is entirely His. You are completely free of it. It is gone, done, finished, over. It is as if it never happened. Through the Love of God, you and the other person are both now and forever free.

Fox then concludes with a surprise. He says get up and go about your business. Do not repeat this act of forgiveness. You have done it once. To do it a second time would be to repudiate everything you have already done.

Thereafter, whenever the memory of the offender or the offense comes into your mind, briefly give the person to God and dismiss the thought. Do this every time the thought comes back. After a while, Fox insists, it will recur less and less often until you forget it completely.

In addition, you may think of the situation that caused the resentment as having happened to someone other than yourself. Indeed, it did. You are not the person you were then. That was you at that time, not the you who exists today. You are recovered;

you have been reborn. The things that happened to the you of then did not happen to the you of today.

I think of resentments as coming in three sizes: Little (also known as Mild), Fairly Big, and Really Big. Recently I discovered that I sometimes acquire a resentment of a more subtle nature. It's a variation of the Really Big variety. However, it doesn't suddenly erupt as a result of someone doing something really horrendous that upsets me in a big way. Rather, it evolves slowly.

Someone with whom I have repeated contact over a fairly long period of time irritates me over and over again. At first it's only a minor dissatisfaction, but over time it becomes increasingly more annoying. Eventually it really upsets me. But, because of the way it sneaked up on me, I don't recognize it as the big, fat resentment it has become. As a result, not realizing its true nature, instead of dealing with it appropriately, I unwittingly carry it around for an inordinate length of time. But when I finally recognize it for what it is, it sure feels good to be rid of it.

Victims of life. Resentments aren't the only way we end up in the victim role. We get there as the result of an unhappy childhood, an unsatisfactory job or marriage, lack of money, poor health, an unfriendly town or neighborhood, disagreeable relatives, unruly children, and uncooperative parents or teachers. In fact, just about any person or thing we can think of to blame for our life.

We also hear a lot about how far too many of us spend our lives unhappy because we didn't come up to the expectations of our parents, many of whom are long-since dead. Less frequently discussed is how many of us are chronically unhappy because we don't come up to the expectations of our children, many of whom delight in showing us their disapproval.

All of this is what makes "victimhood" so popular. As victims, we aren't responsible for our lives. We blame someone else. However, this statement is true for me, and it's true for every one else: My life is my responsibility. The circumstances of my life don't determine the quality of my life; the quality of my life is determined by my reaction to circumstances.

Many people find it easier to have no goals or aspirations. To them, *Let Go and Let God* means "Sit back and wait for God to do something." *Easy Does It* means "Relax, do nothing."

Don is such a person. He's in his fifties. He just returned from visiting his wife who moved to another state because she doesn't want to live with him any more. In answer to my question, he says she is "70% the reason" they are not living together; he's "30%." He doesn't know what she dislikes about him except that they are "very different." For example, he "eats different."

Don isn't working. He prayed for a job, and that same day a man called and offered him the position of manager of the Western Region of a sizable company. He isn't sure if that call was the answer to his prayer, and he isn't sure whether he should take the job or maybe look around some more. It's a major problem for Don.

He was also concerned that he drinks several quarts of Pepsi every day. Before he left to visit his wife, I suggested he cut the amount in half and then start tapering off. He cut it in half, but hasn't progressed any further for no particular reason. I asked him what he wants to do with the rest of his life. He doesn't know. I asked what he wanted on his tombstone. He said, "That he was a good man." I asked how he would define "a good man." He wasn't sure. Don doesn't want anything in particular. To my knowledge, he helps no one, calls no one, doesn't know the meaning of the word sponsor, has no goals or aspirations and doesn't recognize his lack of them. He's a victim of life.

It's almost impossible to help victims. In spite of what they say, they don't want change; they want sympathy. They want others to understand and agree with their difficult plight.

As for resentments, there apparently are advantages to retaining them. Like Jim J.'s unhappy wife who likes to remind him repeatedly of his infidelity and his former girlfriend, but who refuses to go to Al-Anon.

Many people use this sort of emotional blackmail. They get more joy out of punishing the other person than in being happy themselves. They hold on to a false sense of superiority in keeping the focus on the other person's faults and errors. Besides, if they appeared happy, others might think their behavior no longer mattered, and there's no telling what they'd do then.

As a newcomer to Al-Anon said, "I certainly don't want to do anything to make *him* feel better," even though she herself must go on feeling miserable. Many of us exhibit this same behavior but lack her degree of insight and honesty.

Also, it seems important to hold on to the idea that, as the injured party, we are obviously right, and the person who caused our distress is therefore obviously wrong. To give in now might be interpreted as an admission that we might have been at least partially wrong, and we certainly don't want that!

As we grow in the program, we realize that assigning blame is not only a waste of time, it is a serious impediment to emotional independence and peace of mind. It really doesn't matter who is to blame. That's not the important question. The important question is who will be the first to take a leadership role in recovery? Who will be the first to surrender, to call a truce, to bring joy and love back into the relationship?

Instead of competing to see who will win the argument, let the spirit of competition determine who will be the first to give in, the first to accept the fact of the situation and change it. In a very important sense, the first to surrender wins.

On the other hand, it can be quite disconcerting and embarrassing to suddenly realize that while you continued to complain about your partner, they got busy working their program and are now obviously far ahead of you in recovery.

As mentioned earlier, the victim role can be addictive. I grew up with a close relative who enjoyed the victim role all her life. She laughed a high-pitched, semi-hysterical laugh much of the time—until old age. Before that, she laughed and displayed a sort of happy-martyr attitude as she recited a litany of dire things that had happened to her. My mother used to tell us how difficult our relative's life was and how sorry we should feel for her.

The laughter completely disappeared when she grew old. Still the victim, she was now openly bitter. Everything about her life had been someone else's fault.

Victims of our children. Each of us comes by our tendency toward victimhood quite naturally. As infants, when in distress, whether from hunger, pain, or whatever, we cried until someone proved their love for us by taking care of our problem. If they didn't come quickly enough, we screamed.

Years later when hurt, we ran home to mother to kiss it and make it well. Still later when we had problems at school, our parents straightened things out with the teacher. As we grew older, and the law or our creditors gave us trouble, our parents took care of the problem.

In this way they proved their love for us. The more upset they became when we had a problem, the more they demonstrated their love, right? "I can't be happy until you're happy too," was their tune. We loved it and stayed in the victim role while they felt disloyal if they didn't continue to feel "concerned about our welfare."

While many thousands of parents never learn a different approach, other thousands come to Al-Anon and learn a far more comfortable and more effective way to live. Problems in various children's lives, of which I am personally aware, have included, diabetes; obesity; a vast array of other serious medical problems; decreased mental capacity; serious auto accidents with multiple fractures, lacerations and coma; jail and penitentiary sentences; spousal abuse; sexual abuse; child abuse; poverty, hunger and homelessness; infidelity, desertion, divorces and separations; extreme drug addiction; psychotic states; and more.

Amazingly, parents of these children have learned to lead more comfortable, more productive lives by becoming active, enthusiastic, participating, long-term members of Al-Anon. And subsequently their children have often dramatically recovered from the above situations. But this happened only after the parents got out of the way, stopped putting energy into the problem, stopped "helping" their children, stopped doing what wasn't working and became willing to try something different.

Naomi D. changed the way she communicates with her daughter, and their entire relationship changed. Here is her story as she related it to me.

In 1992, Naomi was referred to Al-Anon by an OA friend following a tearful recitation of her concern for her wayward daughter, Diane. Previously, Naomi said she had been extremely tense when talking to her daughter, always searching for the right words to get her into recovery, and always trying to make the decision that would prove to her daughter that she loved her. Nothing ever worked.

Eventually Naomi's sponsor helped her see the truth about her behavior. She was doing what she was doing, not because her actions were helping her daughter—they weren't—but because she felt too uncomfortable doing nothing. Naomi accepted the fact that everything she did was based on selfish motives. She became willing to allow her daughter to take the consequences of her own behavior and thereby perhaps learn what she needed to learn.

Naomi now listens to her daughter, acknowledges how difficult life must be for her, then uses what she refers to as the broken record technique. No matter how much Diane argues, Naomi repeatedly responds with a statement such as. "No, Diane, it's not an option for you to stay here. Where would you like me to take you?" Formerly, she couldn't say no without explaining her decision and hoping her daughter would understand. This merely opened the matter to further negotiations which Diane always won.

She no longer asks, "How are you?" Rather, she says, "It's good to hear your voice." This is often followed by "Diane, I'm sorry, but for my own serenity, I can't afford to hear the details. I love you. I respect you, and I know you'll make the right decision."

Naomi says she has given up the right to tell Diane she needs to change. She realizes that the more she tries to control Diane, the more she is under Diane's control. If how Naomi feels or what she does next depends on whether or not Diane does or does not do whatever Naomi wants her to do, then Naomi is under Diane's control.

Naomi says she sent Diane to college to get an education, but she came back two years later with an addiction which has put her in jail several times. This, Naomi says, is not what she had in mind.

Recently, about the time Naomi was convinced that Diane was dead, she finally heard from her. She was in a homeless shelter trying to decide between two different recovery homes. Two days later Diane complained that she had chosen the wrong one. This brought Naomi back into the picture. She frantically tried to solve the problem in order to keep her daughter in treatment. At this point her sponsor told her:

> If Diane is going to make a program work, it will work. It's not the place, it's the question, "Is she ready to surrender to getting well someone else's way?" When Diane's desire for life becomes greater than her desire for drugs, her recovery will begin, and not until then. Diane needs to start somewhere. When you are in the army, you do army. You don't negotiate army. Diane wants to do Diane. That's her disease. She insists on negotiating, and she's not in a position to negotiate.

Diane left the recovery home after two days. Naomi is grateful that Diane once had three months recovery in a Twelve Step program. As a result, she knows what recovery is and where she can find it— whenever she's ready for it.

Meanwhile, Naomi moves on, living her own life while Diane does whatever she is destined to do with hers.

Transactional analysis. There is a different, often unrecognized but extremely common, form of victimhood which is understandable according to Transactional Analysis (TA). TA says every communication (transaction) between two people can be analyzed to show an interplay between or among what is referred to as the Adult, the Parent, and the Child.

During childhood, we each acquired our impression of who we are from our Parents. Whether our Nurturing Parent or our Critical Parent had the greater impact determined whether we ended up as a Natural Child with healthy self-esteem or as a Not-OK Child with low self-esteem.

Essentially, these five entities (Nurturing Parent and Critical Parent, Natural Child and Not-OK Child, and Adult) correspond to five of the many voices in our heads.

In every conversation, these voices play the role described by their name. The Adult is a mature individual with common sense and intelligence. The Child is immature and needs direction, discipline, guidance and love. The Parent verbally and non-verbally provides these things to the Child.

In healthy, adult relationships, this interplay works fine. If the husband stays home from work with a bad cold or flu, he falls into the needy Child role, and his spouse, in the Adult role, takes care of him. If the kids misbehave when they come home from school, she changes to the Critical Parent. Later that night, as a sex partner, she may assume the playful Natural Child role.

This system works well as long as each person involved in the transaction (the communication) assumes the appropriate role to fit the situation and the circumstances. Difficulties arise when either party, or both, take inappropriate roles. Some people, for example, having been raised in a home with a great deal of fighting, can't stand shouting or other displays of anger. As a result, when their spouse raises their voice, they assume the frightened Not-OK Child role. The spouse now comes across as the scolding Critical Parent and thus the dominant one in the relationship.

The less-dominant (Not-OK Child) partner hates this relationship but, feeling not-OK and childlike, can't verbalize their feelings, and they become passive aggressive. He or she thinks, "I'll do what you say, but I won't enjoy it—and *neither will you!*"

Both partners are now victims—each of the other's behavior. Neither has emotional independence.

Problems of this type are certainly not limited to couples. Fear of another person for whatever reason, real or imagined, prevents adult individuals from interacting in a mature, Adult-to-Adult manner. Think of how you revert to the Child role when stopped by a Highway Patrol Officer. Do you always maintain your Adult status when you talk to your boss, doctor, lawyer, mother, father, sponsor or an overbearing neighbor? Or do you, because of fear, give away your emotional independence, your ability to choose how you are going to feel when dealing with a perceived authority figure?

Recognizing a communication problem is one thing; doing something constructive about it is quite another matter. In the following chapters we'll discuss what to do.

6. TECHNIQUES

In the book *Alcoholics Anonymous,* perhaps no single suggestion has more to do with maintaining emotional sobriety than the admonition "We have ceased fighting anything and anybody." That apparently means *any* thing and *any* body—all the way from total strangers to the people we work and live with every day.

We accomplish this unusual feat by maintaining our emotional independence. And we maintain our emotional independence by not allowing others to control our emotions, by not, for instance, allowing them to make us angry. As mentioned earlier, in *How To Argue And Win Every Time,* Gerry Spence states emphatically that people have only as much power over us as we give them. Indeed, the main thrust of his book seems to be to not fear an opponent because he or she has only as much power over us as we willingly give him or her.

I'm almost embarrassed when I think of the number of times over the years when I foolishly gave my power to people I didn't even like. Today, on the other hand, it feels great when I manage to rise above the situation and the other person's behavior. I accomplish this by refusing to submit to their implied request that I become upset. By staying emotionally independent, I maintain control over my emotional state. And by remaining calm, I often have a positive and sometimes a profound effect on the overall situation and the other person's behavior.

This has been my experience and the experience of others who have been willing to try it. The first, the most crucial step, as repeatedly mentioned, is to remain aware of having a choice. The other person can make us angry *only* if we agree. If he or she wants to argue, and we realize that arguing with them is a waste of time, we do *not* have to argue. They can not *make* us argue. We, not the other person, are in charge of our emotional state. Our emotional choices are our responsibility, not the responsibility of that person or that situation.

It's normal to have emotions, to feel, for example, appropriate anger. But it's not necessary to let anger control us. An old Chinese proverb tells us if we don't control our feelings, our feelings will control us. Anger isn't harmful, it's what we do with anger that causes problems.

Here are randomly chosen examples of things we can do rather than allow our emotions to be controlled by a unpleasant situation or a difficult person.

Reframe.   We can control our emotions by consciously or unconsciously reframing the situation. When something distasteful happens, my usual reaction is determined by the voices in my head. I hear shouts such as, "He can't talk to me like that! That's not fair; I won't stand for it!" I then react accordingly.

By reframing this picture, instead of acting as my emotions suggest, I look at the situation from a different perspective. Instead of instantly reacting to the first thoughts that come into my head, I ask, "Is this really worth getting upset over? Is it all that important? Is it more important than my serenity?" As I ask questions like this, the situation doesn't change, but I change. I change how I perceive the situation—and thereby change my attitude toward it.

As a result, I am able to respond to the situation in a more mature, more sensible, more effective manner, a manner superior to what my emotions would have had me do based on how *they* first saw the situation. More and more, as I develop the habit of doing this, I begin to do it automatically, unthinkingly, unconsciously.

One day in San Francisco, I got an embarrassing lesson in reframing. But, instead of me reframing the picture, it reframed itself.

As I drove up a hill, a car sat in my lane at the top of the hill waiting for the light to change. The distance and my rate of speed were such that I knew the light would turn green and the car would be moving by the time I got there.

The light changed. The car didn't move. I began to slow down. He still didn't move. A crash was becoming imminent, and I thought, "You crazy fool! Why don't you get out of there?"

At the last minute, I hit the brakes. As my car screeched to a halt, I looked up. Racing up the hill from the other side, was what the other driver had been watching, an ambulance and two fire trucks with flashing red lights.

This is not the kind of reframing lesson I enjoy.

Many recovering people are either unwilling or unable to reframe their problems. More likely, they are unaware of having a choice in the matter of maintaining their emotional independence.

For example: The phone rang as we sat down for breakfast. The caller made it clear, as callers often do, that he was calling only because his sponsor insisted that he do so.

He said he was going crazy. He'd recently gotten sober in a long-term recovery home. He ranted and raved because his wife wouldn't talk to him. She and their two children had forced him out of the house because of his drinking, and now she was proceeding with a divorce. All of this in spite of how wonderfully he was doing with his beautiful, several days of sobriety. "This time it's different," he insisted. "I've never felt like this before!"

As one might expect, he, the alcoholic, couldn't see the problem from his wife's point of view. He visualized the situation utilizing the same alcoholic brain that kept him drinking all through their marriage. Typically alcoholic, he was judging himself by his intentions, while his spouse was judging him by his behavior.

Commonly, two people having such divergent viewpoints try to talk things out. Sad to say, talking often makes the situation worse. But when either partner is willing to listen to a sponsor or a third party, and look at the situation from a different perspective, dramatic changes can take place. As he and I talked, he became willing, at least for the moment, to look at the situation from his wife's perspective. He changed his tune, changed his way of communicating, and his resentment subsided.

Often I find myself in this same sort of situation. I'm upset because of Max's behavior, and I try to get her to change so I'll feel better. The trick is to accept responsibility for my own feelings regardless of what she does or doesn't do, to keep my focus on me and my emotions rather than on her and her behavior. But I can't get my focus on me until I first get it off her.

It's like the picture of the pretty young girl and the old hag. See Fig. 1. 1.

If you see one person in the picture, say, the old hag, and your partner sees the young girl, you will not be able to see what your part- ner sees until you give up what you see. Both people are there in the picture, but you can see only one or the other, not both at the same time. In like manner, you can't see a situation from another's viewpoint until you first give up your fascination with your own viewpoint.

Don't join them! While most of us don't unquestioningly accept other people's opinions, we all too readily accept their negative emotions. We become magnets. Without thinking, we react in kind to negative people. We go along with them in whatever mood they are in. If they are angry, we are angry; if they shout, we shout. I have no idea why it is so easy to mimic others in this way. Why aren't we as quick to copy the behavior of people who are happy and joyful?

When facing an upset individual, joining them in their upset state is the worst thing we can do.

At times like this, it is especially necessary to maintain our emotional independence. If we display a sense of calm, they may calm down. Certainly nothing is gained by imitating them. They're already disturbed and unhappy. Why double the number of disturbed and unhappy people, and thus make a bad situation worse?

John and Mary, for example, run a family business together. He doesn't think she does her share of the work, and she doesn't think he understands what needs to be done. Any time she tries to talk to him, he becomes defensive and upset. She immediately joins him in his negative mood. They have a fight, and the problem is now worse than before.

You get the same effect when you speak to a practicing alcoholic about his drinking. He or she immediately becomes defensive and argumentative. By responding in kind, you also become defensive and argumentative. A heated discussion takes place. The alcoholic drinks even more and blames it on you. Now you are both more upset than before.

Recently a fellow told me about two important observations he had made about communicating with his strong-willed, alcoholic partner who always *wins* when they argue. He said he was amazed to discover that, first, he is the one who sets the tone in their relationship. If he acts warm and friendly, she acts warm and friendly; if he acts distant and uncommunicative, she acts distant and uncommunicative.

Second, he has noticed that after she says something mean and hurtful to him, she listens to his response so that she can top it by coming back with something even more hostile. This upsets him further, and he becomes more defensive or hostile. And off they go, the conversation (if you can call it that) getting louder and louder and progressively more intense and hurtful.

On the other hand, he has found that he can turn this negative charade into something positive. When she says something mean and hurtful, he doesn't react in kind. She isn't able to top what he says if he says nothing. Or she has no retort if he says something bland such as the Al-Anon reply, *You could be right.* As a result, she hears only herself and the hurtful remark that she had already made. Now she often comes back later to retract what she said.

Someone has said that in interpersonal relationships, it's the weak person who has all the power. This is an example of that truth.

Don't walk out. If you find yourself getting increasingly more upset, or if your partner insists on talking at a time when you're absolutely not in the mood to listen, don't get angry and walk out. Briefly state your feelings, then make an appointment. "I'm sorry. I'm too upset to talk about it right now. But I am willing to discuss it with you when I get home from work tonight. Can we agree on that?"

Have no expectations. Our emotional distress often arises from our expectations of others—either expecting too much and not getting it, or expecting too little and getting it.

As was said at a recent AA workshop, "If you wish to effect a change in another person, you must first do what you would have them do." And, "Expectations are precursors to resentments."

Write down five things (for example: courtesy, kindness, understanding) that you would like to receive from your partner. Now give those things to him or her. As you continue to do this, they will be impressed by your new behavior, and you may be impressed to find them responding in kind to you.

Beware the trivia. It's often the little things that bother us. The "tyranny of trivia" one A.A. member calls it. Sitting in never-ending judgment of people, places, things and situations keeps us annoyed by facts that are essentially none of our business.

For example, by growing up in a neighborhood drug store, I learned that the customer is king. Now I get upset when I go to the new, neighborhood, chain drug store down the street where the clerks have not yet received this training. They think of customers as interfering with their routine activities. They talk to each other and ignore the most important person in the store, me.

More recently I got upset at the supermarket. The male clerk was too busy talking to the girl clerks to give me the attention I deserved. He didn't pack my purchases, and when I started doing it myself, he tried to take over. As I walked away, he talked to the other customers and clerks as if I were a crabby old man who caused the whole incident. (Maybe he was right.)

I'm impressed with the way my computer's word processor program automatically and immediately points out, and sometimes even corrects my typing errors. I wish I had a similar program following me around through life automatically and immediately correcting my words, speech, and behavior as fast as this program corrects my spelling. It would save me a lot of trouble, anguish and embarrassment.

Forget on purpose. It's not denial, but if there is absolutely nothing you can do about a situation, and it isn't worth being upset over, why give it mental time and energy by repeatedly ruminating about it? Instead, make a conscious decision to put it out of your mind. Choose to think instead about something else, anything else, the Serenity Prayer, for instance.

Accept irreconcilable differences. What can you do when you and your partner disagree on a matter, and you can't work it out? One or the other refuses to see a counselor or a third party, or makes it a waste of time if you do. When you try to discuss the problem, nothing constructive happens, and each side uses the same words and rationalizations they've used over and over in the past. You start to argue, and both end up more frustrated and resentful than before.

This is particularly true when you personally are affected in a significant way by your partner's attitude and behavior. Examples of problems of this type include matters of money, sex, kids and social life.

Psychologists and other professionals tell us we should talk out our differences, and assertion training tells us we will feel better if we make our feelings heard even if we don't get our way. We are told we must do this for our personal emotional benefit only. If we expect the other party to change in order to please us, we set ourselves up for more trouble. We now know they know their behavior bothers us, and they continue to do it anyway!

Of course, acceptance is ultimately the answer. Acceptance is neither approval, nor submission. We simply accept the facts of the situation. Then we make a decision and exercise a choice.

What is the goal? Is it to get the other to admit they are wrong, and you are right? Or is your goal simply to feel better?

If the former, begin by asking yourself why you need to have it your way. Try role reversal. Assume your partner's role. See what it feels like. If you think you are being manipulated, you might decide, O.K., I'll let him have his way—*this* time. In this manner, in a certain sense, you take charge of the situation by *letting* your partner behave as he or she is behaving.

You'll feel even better if you let your partner know that from now on, however they act, whatever they do is up to them. Henceforth, they, not you, are responsible for their behavior.

Of course, it's always good to talk to God before you do anything. Pray, ask for guidance, be clear as to your motive, leave the outcome entirely up to God, then proceed. In my experience, if I do a thing for the right motive (love is always a right motive), and leave the result entirely up to God, things turn out the way they are supposed to.

Whenever possible, it helps to add a bit of humor, or to say things that will make the other person feel good about themselves. Like the story of black paint. If the situation is black, you can't make it white. But every time you add white paint to a can of black paint, like adding cream to black coffee, the mixture becomes less black. So it is with a difficult situation; it becomes whiter and whiter with the addition of a little humor or encouragement.

Above all, don't be passive-aggressive. Don't acquiesce for now but get back at your partner later. And don't go along with it in private but complain about it to your friends. Take a leadership role in your own life while your partner is doing whatever they are doing with their life.

Don't fight no matter how the other reacts to your new approach. Quietly state that you have heard that you will feel better if you let your feelings (resentments, for example) be known. Then calmly (using "I" sentences, not "You" sentences) state how you feel. But, as mentioned above, don't expect your statement to produce a change in your partner's behavior. In fact, it's wise to make it clear to them that they do not have to change in any way.

Such a statement helps you to not expect a change, and, paradoxically, it makes change more likely. For some reason, people only change for the better when they feel accepted as they are. Having been told that they don't need to change, they feel free to change and to think of it as their own idea. Furthermore, being thus freed of a sense of responsibility for your feelings, they will feel less threatened when you express them in the future.

Max and I have often ended our differences by agreeing, "I'll put up with you if you'll put up with me." Also, when my irritation comes from the fact that Max is not doing something I want her to do, I ask myself what I would do if she were no longer with me. With her theoretically out of the picture, I look for other solutions. Commonly this simply means taking care of the matter myself. As time goes on, I find myself doing this increasingly more often and avoiding many of the former uncomfortable situations and resentments.

By doing all these things, you will, one day at a time, be following God's will rather than your partner's. You'll be hooked into God and the lesson to be learned. You'll be saying, "Okay God, if this is what you want me to do today, I'll do it for *You*."

Live in the answer. Live in the program, not in the problem. This is easy to say and even easier to forget. Many of us are like John and Shirley. They both worked active recovery programs until a serious medical problem developed. Naturally, they began to work on the problem. Gradually this took more and more of their time, and they couldn't get to as many meetings. As time went by, they devoted still more time and worry to the medical problem. This allowed even less time for their recovery programs.

Sadly, the worse the problem became, the more they needed what they felt they no longer had time for. Because their minds were filled with the problem, they didn't recognize their need, and they became sicker and sicker. Now they had two problems: the health problem and the dry drunk syndrome which develops in alcoholics (and other twelve-step people) who don't go to meetings

Had they had time for a meeting, they might have heard the young lady say, "When I stopped living in the problem and started living in the answer, the problem went away." In this case, the problem wouldn't have gone away, but they could have felt a great deal better while dealing with it—and perhaps dealt with it more effectively.

It doesn't take a major medical problem like this to cause this kind of situation. Couples get into trouble any time one or both focuses excessive amounts of time and energy on any problem they see as demanding their attention. This can be anything from making more money to going to school or raising children—anything that keeps them in the problem and out of their recovery program.

Others appear addicted to their misery as they energize and keep their problem alive by dwelling on it. Henry lives in a sober-living home. His wife and kids won't talk to him. They have a restraining order to keep him away because he threatened to kill his wife during his last insane bout with alcohol. He spends his time pleading with his wife to remove the restraining order and stop the divorce. He gets so upset working on this problem that he can't keep from drinking! But that doesn't keep him from thinking that this time it would be different if she'd simply let bygones be bygones. He can't get his eyes off what he sees as the problem. Henry reminds me of the definition of an alcoholic that says an alcoholic is a person who drinks to solve problems created by drinking.

Joe is another example. He's done one stupid thing after another at work. Now he is about to be fired. Although he's been around the program for several years, he's done nothing regarding the Steps or a recovery program. Instead, he obsesses on his problems: his boss, his job, his allegedly inadequate sponsor and the many people who are angry with him.

Marc does the same thing. He talks only and at length about his many terrible problems at work. Although he attends A.A. meetings regularly, he has never done the Steps. He spends so much time complaining about his problems that he has no time for anything like that.

Prioritize. Many people have little or no emotional sobriety because emotional sobriety is such a low priority item for them. They value their resentments over their serenity. From their resentments they get their energy.

The other day I met a man I wouldn't call sober even though his length of time without a drink was longer than mine. He delighted in telling me about the many things that upset him, including the A.A. meeting he'd just walked out of.

He said he was having trouble with a relationship. When I suggested Al-Anon, he told me his favorite resentment. Many years before, when he was still drinking heavily, "Al-Anon told my partner to leave me, and I've hated them ever since."

I've heard that same sentiment expressed several times around A.A. "How dare they tell my partner to consider looking out for himself instead of putting up with my drunken behavior forever?"

Emotional sobriety demands from us both a high priority and a leadership role in maintaining it. Here is a story Sue W. told me about how she put a high priority on her emotional sobriety and what she has done to obtain and maintain it.

Sue said she had always thought of herself as God's little helper, always trying to make everyone happy and always knowing what was good for everyone else. She described her husband as prone to mood swings, criticism and depression. Never knowing what to expect next, she said she stayed in a constant state of readiness and alert. On the other hand, she said he soon forgot his displays of unpleasantness while she felt wounded and upset for a whole weekend.

Eventually she realized that, while she couldn't change his behavior, she could change her reaction to it, and she began to develop techniques for doing so. Initially she got a rubber baseball bat and worked off her frustrations beating her bed. At other times, especially in the car, when she felt upset by what he was saying, she visualized his words as spewing out into the air, then falling on her and having a toxic effect if she allowed them to remain there. To counteract this, she busied herself carefully brushing them off the sleeves of her jacket and the legs of her pants.

Sue said she remembered Max saying she routinely asked herself three questions: Is it important? Is there anything I can do about it? Is it any of my business? Initially, Sue said she felt that all her thoughts were important, and with enough persistence she could change any situation. Furthermore, since she was only trying to be helpful, everything was her business. To suggest otherwise she considered kind of rude.

Today, before getting involved in what otherwise might turn into a heated debate, she asks herself Max's three questions. Previously she didn't know she had a choice.

Sue now writes letters to God to let Him know what is going on in her life. Over time, she says, the messages are turning into letters of gratitude. She is grateful, for instance, that she is learning to patiently listen to her husband instead of abruptly giving him unsolicited advice that in the past had always provoked another argument.

She says she's also grateful to have learned that just because she thinks she's right, doesn't mean he is automatically wrong. Listening to him and understanding his family history and perspective, she can see now how he might think the way he does. Now, instead of getting upset, she says to herself, "That's just the way he is," and she tries to show him the same courtesy she wants to receive from him.

Today Sue admits that without her husband she would not have acquired many of the gifts of the program such as compassion, unconditional love, tolerance, and a feeling of independence. She says, "I'm grateful that I no longer have to give another human being control over my feelings and emotions. I've sure come a long way."

7. MORE TECHNIQUES

Declare your emotional independence. This requires a drastic change in personal philosophy, a change from, *"It's okay for me to be upset as long as I have a good reason";* to, *"I accept full responsibility for my feelings, my attitudes, and I will no longer blame them on the behavior of others."*

It means giving up what we have been taught all our lives—that we should be upset simply because the person we love is upset. That's a particularly foolish and impractical concept, and it certainly isn't love.

Emotional independence, on the other hand, means such things as:

- Taking a leadership role in our own feelings, thinking, actions and attitude.
- Not fighting even when the other is angry and trying to provoke a fight.
- No longer waiting to see how someone else feels before deciding how to feel.
- Responding rather than reacting.
- Deciding to have a good day no matter how others feel or act.
- Realizing that being upset accomplishes nothing of value, and isn't worth the bother.
- Realizing that we spend more of our lives living with ourselves than with anyone else; therefore, it's important to be happy and comfortable being who we are.
- No longer using our emotional state to manipulate other people's behavior, or to

punish them for past misbehavior—no more pouting.

- Not letting our life be a reflection of what's going on in someone else's life—each of us is in charge of our own lives with a distinct boundary between us.
- Emotional independence means realizing that the problem we say is upsetting us has only as much power as we give it.
- It means saying, "I'm going to have a good day today no matter what anyone else says or does."
- It means taking a real leadership role in my own life. As is said in Al-Anon: *The emphasis begins to be lifted from the alcoholic and placed where we do have some power—over our own lives.*[1]

Naomi used her Al-Anon and O.A. programs to walk through the following particularly difficult situation. Although she hadn't heard from her oldest son, whom she idolized, she wasn't too concerned because she knew he was in the process of moving to Northern California and would no doubt call when he got settled. However, when she got home from work one evening, her husband informed her that two weeks earlier, Ron, her twenty-five year old son, had been murdered. His body had been dumped in a lake with all identification removed.

Now, two weeks later and in possession of all of Ron's personal effects, the murderer had been

---

[1] *Understanding Ourselves and Alcoholism,* p. 5.

picked up for drunk driving. Ten years after having been sentenced to 30 years to life in a Texas prison, he was paroled to live in California. Fourteen days into his parole he needed a car. Not only did he take Ron's car and possessions, he, for no reason, took Ron's life.

The trial began five years later. Naomi who, prior to Al-Anon, had never been able to open her mouth in public, was called as a witness. She says that with the support of her husband, sponsor and friends in the program, she was able to "...speak up in court and let them know my son through me. Somehow that felt like I was honoring him." The man was convicted of murder in the first degree and sentenced to San Quentin.

Naomi says she was never angry at God for what happened to her son. She prefers to believe that a man not doing God's will murdered her son. She also believes that a way to honor her son's memory is to not play over and over again in her mind the tragic way in which he died. She says, "He lived it only once, and I believe to honor him is to live the best life I can. I know that is what he would want for me. God has granted me the serenity to accept that which I cannot change."

Assume it's a communication problem. No matter what the problem seems to be, treat it like a communication problem. Remember that a measure of the effectiveness of communication is the result it produces.

If you are not getting the result you want in communicating with another individual, assume that you are not communicating effectively. Take responsibility for the situation. Instead of blaming the other person, blame your communication skill, or lack thereof. You have a much greater chance of improving your communication skill than you have of changing that person. As one of the poets said, "A man convinced against his will, is of the same opinion still."

Take on the task of finding out how to both verbally and non-verbally communicate with the other person in such a manner that you will be happy with the final result. Life consists of one communication event after another. Assume that your problem is one more such situation. Accept the challenge of solving it by communicating more effectively.

Over the years, I've had many opportunities to do this. I know it works. It has changed the atmosphere or mood in my home, and on many occasions it has resulted in a dramatic improvement in the lives of people with whom I work in recovery.

Throughout life, most of us receive no training related to communicating effectively. Yet, what could be more important?

Get angry. There's nothing wrong, nothing abnormal about getting angry. What matters is what we do with the anger. Anger is energizing. Denying anger, suppressing it, pretending it doesn't exist causes all sorts of emotional and physical illnesses which in turn keep psychologists, psychiatrists and other doctors busy much of the time.

Anger commonly results in action—action that is either destructive or constructive. For some reason, probably habit and emotional immaturity, many of us display our anger in destructive activities such as gossiping, hitting, shouting, blaming, name-calling, fighting, etc. But anger dissipated in constructive activities such as participation in political, academic, social, environmental and legal activities demonstrates emotional maturity and is far more comfortable for everyone concerned.

Simply sharing one's feelings honestly with an appropriate person or group is a common example of dealing with anger (resentments) constructively.

The power behind destructive anger makes a bad situation worse. The power behind constructive anger is directed toward correcting or improving a bad situation. One's thinking changes from "Isn't this awful?" to "What can be done about this?"

An example might be when we are annoyed because an A.A. or similar meeting is deteriorating. Cross-talk is increasing, people continually bring in outside issues, and there's less and less basic program. Such a situation can be upsetting. But instead of gossiping about the attendees and complaining about the meeting, we can put our energy into starting a new, bigger, happier meeting that adheres to the traditions and is a joy to attend.

An even simpler constructive approach is to deliberately share in a positive manner any time a meeting takes a negative turn. In other words, model the behavior we wish to promote.

An advantage to this approach is that we end up feeling good about ourselves. At least such has been my experience. We actually do get back what we put out. "Whatsoever a man soweth, that shall he also reap".[2]

Here, in her own words, is what Judy R. did with her anger.

Before Al-Anon, I never understood the word "respond." Neither did I relate responding to emotional sobriety. Thank God, Al-Anon is a program of progress, not perfection. If this were not true, I would have failed many times over, would have become discouraged and would have chucked the whole idea of working a program.

I am grateful to God that there is no failure in the Al-Anon program. If I don't get the message the first time, my God always provides me another opportunity to put the Steps to work and to grow.

A recent weekend provided just such an occasion. On returning home from the movies one evening with a friend, I found our street filled with cars and a great number of wandering teenagers involved in a noisy graduation party. My adrenaline began to rush and I became angry.

It was obvious that a great deal of drinking and drugging was taking place, and one more time I began to react, project, assume, and do everything our Al-Anon

---

[2] Bible, Galatians 6:7

"Don'ts" tell us not to do. While locking up for the night, I heard voices in our side yard and saw a young, very drunk, young woman with her pants down about to eliminate herself in our yard.

Anger hardly describes my emotional state. I raged, I called the police, and I spent a sleepless night talking to the committee in my head. Working my program was not on my mind. I was too busy setting myself up for a continuation of the insanity.

The next morning, tired and still angry, I went outside to see if there had been any property damage. I found trash in the yard. I picked it up and placed it in the yard across the street where the party had continued long into the night. After all, it was their responsibility to pick up the party attendees' trash. (Our neighborhood had had many problems with the alcoholic father and his son who lived there.)

Placing the trash in the neighbor's yard was a real mistake. The young man came running out of the house shouting and calling me names. I *reacted* with my old behavior. I argued with a drug user with a hangover, trying to show him how right I was. You know the pattern.

Later, when I realized that I had *reacted* and had not *responded* (I still needed to set boundaries and establish, for me, what was and was not acceptable behavior), I decided to write a letter to the mother of the family.

I wrote the letter and shared it with my sponsor, with a recovering alcoholic and with two secular people. I listened to their suggestions and rewrote the letter removing some of the passages. Then I hand-delivered the letter. To my shock and dismay, the mother wadded the letter up and threw it on the lawn.

Now I felt was the time to let the situation go. It was easy for me to do because writing the letter had allowed me to share my feelings, set boundaries, and establish acceptable and unacceptable behavior for me. I was free.

But that's not the end. Within a short period of time, the raging son and mother came across the street to my house with the crumpled letter in hand. I had only moments to throw up a quick prayer asking God to give me love, compassion, understanding, and the ability to respond, not react. I asked Him to give me the grace to work the program I had failed to work the first time.

It is amazing what God does when you trust Him and turn it over—the first step to emotional sobriety. I listened to a raging son and mother, and when I realized that we were not going to come to a resolution, I did a very strange thing—most unusual for me in such a situation. I said to the young man, "I know you are not going to like what I am going to do, but I am going to do it anyway. I am going to give you a hug."

I put my arms around that young man. He was rigid with rage, but began to relax, and I said to him, "I still have faith in you." I was also given the opportunity to make amends for my irrational behavior.

The young man relaxed with the hug. Funny thing, his attitude and demeanor changed too. He said to me, "You know, had I known what that girl was going to do, I would have stopped her."

The mother turned and said, "You may not have to worry anymore. I'm considering leaving." I replied, "That would be a shame. I would hope you would allow me to take you for coffee sometime before you make that decision."

I meant that response from the bottom of my heart. God did indeed give me what I asked for: love, compassion, understanding, the ability to respond, not react, and the grace to work my program.

My attitude changed. Amazingly, so did theirs. I realized, one more time, my emotional sobriety depends on my being willing to respond rather that to react.

Notice that Judy's changed attitude affected not only her decision regarding what to do, but also the manner in which she did it—and thereby also the outcome.

Give it the short version. And of course, an old technique for dealing with a difficult situation is to remember the so-called Latin proverb *Non illegitimae carborundum*—("Don't let the bastards grind you down.") Give the problem the so-called "Short version of the Serenity Prayer"—"Oh, to Heck with it!"

Don't be defensive—not if you're right, not if you're wrong, not if you're not sure. Defensiveness leads to a fight or injury to one or the other—or both. Nobody wins. Paradoxically, by maintaining a defenseless position, you win.

If you defend yourself, your partner will listen to you for the purpose of deciding what to say next. If, for example, you say nothing, your partner will hear nothing but what they have said. This may allow them to notice how they talk to you.

I seldom remember to remain defenseless until it's too late, but it works when I do. My partner left for her painting class, but walked back in and said in a loud voice, "You took the paint and the palette off the box!" I had no idea what she was talking about, and quietly said so. When she continued to accuse me, I said nothing. She walked through the house, searching and accusing. Finally, I agreed with her and said with a touch of humor and the slightest tinge of sarcasm, "I have no idea what you're talking about, but if something is wrong, it probably is my fault." The encounter ended abruptly. She changed the subject and went on to her class. I had remained defenseless, and it worked.

On another occasion, a neighbor verbally attacked me for walking our dogs along her part of the street. She objected to their droppings. I quietly stated that I discarded the objectionable material into the heavy ground-cover where nature would return it from whence it had come. That only made her more angry and more verbal.

I was wrong; she was right. The law does require that dog-droppings be picked up (and placed in plastic bags, sealed and deposited in trash containers so that, in centuries to come, archeologists can analyze them to learn what we used to feed our dogs, I guess).

The point is, I won the engagement because, no matter what she said, I invited her to "Have a real nice day." By not defending myself, I said and did nothing for which I later had to make amends. I hate making amends.

The same thing happens with sponsees. Occasionally, they get upset or angry when I fail to respond or react to them in precisely the way they think I should. I don't become defensive. By remaining calm, I don't join them in their unhappy emotional state. After they completely finish expressing their feelings, they feel heard and they feel better. I, on the other hand, feel a sense of personal satisfaction at having maintained my emotional independence.

Even lawyers—professionally-trained communicators that they are—sometimes fail the test of defenselessness. The attorney for a pleasant young lady did just that when she brought her father into the office with her. They came to pick up a check they'd been awarded for medical coverage. They thought it belonged to them, and they wanted it. The attorney, however, insisted that, according to the law, it had to go into an escrow account.

A power struggle developed between the father and the college graduate, professionally-trained communicator. Ultimately, the attorney unceremoniously ejected his client's father from the office.

Sadly, this entire situation could have been avoided if the attorney had listened to their story. In the past, they had been seriously mistreated by an attorney. They thought they were being cheated again. The attorney thought he was being called a crook. If he had not become defensive, the final outcome could have been quite different.

Attorneys are not the only professional people who get into power struggles. Such conflicts occur commonly between partners in a relationship where either or both is accustomed to giving orders and detailed instructions at work. Examples include surgeons, military officers, corporate executives, and men and women in all sorts of positions of power and authority.

Conflicts in marriages commonly arise over matters relating to sex, kids, money, in-laws, social life, or just about anything where one partner decides they are right and refuses to be influenced by their supposedly ignorant partner, whom they think of as being wrong. It's quite common to find such couples in severe competition with each other. Each assumes the role of victim of the other's bullheadedness.

Don't argue with someone who is never wrong. I can think of at least a half-dozen couples wherein one or both members are in recovery programs, but only one has ever apologized for being wrong. The other has never made amends for anything. Apparently, in their opinion, they have never been wrong. After an altercation, when one apologizes for having gotten upset, the other quietly accepts the apology, but accepts no responsibility for the altercation itself. They stay in the role of innocent victim of the other's bad behavior.

Nothing is more useless than trying to change someone who thinks they are never wrong. Change for them is too frightening. That's why they refuse to join A.A. or Al-Anon. The only answer I know is to accept the fact that they are the way they are and will never change. Then either leave and be happy, or stay and be happy. But don't stay and complain, or leave and complain. It's a waste of time and energy. You'll only hurt yourself.

Stop focusing on the other person. We insist we feel bad because of the behavior of some other person, when in fact we feel the way we feel because of our conversations with the various "people" both inside and outside our heads.

We talk to the committee in our head and to anyone on the outside who will listen to us. These discussions about the other person's behavior keep us in the victim role. Every time we replay that same old song, we sink a little deeper into self-pity and resentment. To recover, we must stop agreeing with ourselves, and stop trying to get others to agree with us.

A friend made an appointment to talk with me about making amends for a bad situation he had caused, but he said he couldn't get here for several days. During the intervening time, he discussed the situation with the voices in his head. By the time he got here, there was nothing to talk about. He had convinced himself that the other fellow was the sole cause of the problem and had "only gotten what he deserved."

Another friend was telling me how she had been fighting with a neighbor lady, a highly emotional immigrant with many serious problems. The woman had a reputation for fighting with all her neighbors and with anyone willing to do battle with her. My friend talked on and on about how "crazy" she was.

I listened for quite a while, then mentioned that the more insane she described her neighbor, the more insane it seemed to fight with her. Obviously the woman is much more experienced at fighting than my friend will ever be. I suggested that, instead of fighting, my friend might withdraw, stay away; even try, in so far as possible, to be courteous and understanding. Our Big Book says, "We have ceased fighting anything and anybody." As successful members of A.A., we need to maintain our emotional sobriety. And incidentally, we thereby set an example for others.

Learn to listen. Mary Jane called me. She and Henry had returned from a lengthy seminar where they studied and practiced *Imago Therapy*. This is the name of the therapy Hendrix discusses in *Getting The Love You Want, A Guide For Couples* as referred to earlier.

She described some of the things they had learned by saying she was instructed to tell Henry

how she felt about something, and he was to respond *only* by asking for more information. Then he
was to repeat back to her what he thought he heard
her say. She informed him whether or not he was
correct, whether or not what he heard was indeed
what she meant. Again, he repeated what he thought
he heard, and she either agreed or corrected his
impression. Finally he was to ask, "Is there anything
more you want to tell me about this?"

When she answered, "No, that's it," he was to
say, "It sounds like you feel _____," and she was to
either agree or not agree. After they settled on what
her emotion was, he was to ask if she could remember the first time she felt the way she feels now, any
time in her childhood perhaps. If she could, she
went back to that time and discussed it in detail.

By doing this, she found out why she got upset
around this particular situation, while he in turn
discovered he was not the cause of her distress. Not
only was he not the cause of her problem, he was
now a mirror that helped her overcome a hidden,
long-term problem. In the process they both
benefited, and neither was upset at the other.

If the Hendrix method seems artificial and you
can't imagine talking that way, try simply keeping
your mouth shut and listening to your partner.
Instead of being upset at what your partner says,
even though you've heard it many times before,
show interest by nodding, sitting attentively,
making eye contact, offering appropriate simple
comments, and by encouraging your partner to talk.
"Tell me more about that." "How did you feel when
that happened?" "And then what?" You may be
absolutely amazed at what you learn and at the

beneficial effect this has on your partner. Try it out and see for yourself.

Say what you mean.   Hazel didn't want to get sexually involved with a man who was interested in her. She'd informed him that she'd recently broken up with someone else and wasn't yet ready for a new relationship. She had invited him over for dinner, but to keep him from spending the evening and thereby getting too involved, she picked the night of her home group meeting. When he found this unsatisfactory and wanted to spend the evening, she accused him of being "unfair" and insisted that he "ought to respect (her) recovery program." She talked at length trying to make him feel guilty and comparing her recovery program to his.

Obviously, the real problem wasn't who had the better program. It was a matter of her not wanting him to stay, but being unwilling to honestly say so. Instead, she wanted him to guess. Afraid to be assertive, she argued about peripheral issues.

Every once in a while I manage to do it right and am actually assertive rather than aggressive. Max used to take the dogs for a walk each morning, and I took them in the afternoon. She quit when she developed a bout of sciatica. Eventually, although she didn't openly admit it, her condition cleared up.

I continued walking the dogs twice a day, week after week, gradually building up a resentment, but making no comment. Finally, one day while getting dressed to take the dogs out, I commented that I was getting tired of doing this job twice a day, day after day. In other words, instead of blowing up about the unfairness of the situation, and without demanding that she change her behavior in any way, I shared a *feeling*, not an *opinion*. Above all, I did not criticize her.

Neither of us said anything further. The next morning while I was on the treadmill, she said, "I'm taking the dogs out now." She quietly did so, and has continued to do so ever since.

If, while reading about these techniques, you find yourself thinking of reasons why they won't work for you in your particular situation, you may in fact be looking for excuses to not change, to not take charge of your emotional life.

Someone once said, "If you really want to do something, you'll find a way; if you don't, you'll find an excuse."

I hope you change your attitude. I hope you become willing, even eager to change. You can do what many of us have already done. With the help of God, we can do anything.

8. STILL MORE

Just say, "I'd rather not." When someone hassles you to do something you don't want to do, don't offer reasons for not doing it. Giving a reason leads to further discussion and argument. Claiming that you lack the time or money, for example, leads to a debate on how you spend your time or money on other projects.

"I'd rather not," can't be argued with. If they insist on knowing why you'd rather not, simply say, "I'd just rather not." It's honest, and it's one more example of being assertive rather than aggressive or passive.

Max once mentioned at an Al-Anon meeting that she used this technique on me. It sounded good to Winnie E., a then-prominent Al-Anon speaker. Winnie's husband frequently talked her into playing golf when she really didn't want to play. Rather than argue, she might, for example, insist that she had to defrost the refrigerator. While that got her out of playing golf, she ended up having to defrost the refrigerator while her husband was off enjoying himself.

Winnie heard Max, and the next time her husband insisted that she play golf, she said, "No, I'd rather not." Taken by surprise, he demanded, "What the hell do you mean you'd rather not?" Winnie responded with, "I don't know. Max didn't explain it. At a meeting she said, 'When I don't want to do what Paul wants me to do, I simply say,

'I'd rather not.' That's all she told us." Having said that, Winnie enjoyed a quiet day at home.

If the other person tries to make you feel guilty when you use this technique, remember that they are actually saying, "How can you be so selfish as to not want do what I want you to do?"

We mentioned Naomi earlier. Naomi says that before recovery, she had no trouble saying nice things to people. However, that was the only thing she could say. Even if someone asked her a direct question, she could not speak the truth if she thought it might upset them. Sometimes, she said the word "yes" would come out of her mouth when she meant to say "no."

Eventually her sponsor convinced her that if she kept saying yes when she meant to say no, then her yes would have no meaning. She also made her realize that if she asked someone for an honest opinion about herself, she would not want to be lied to just to be kept from having her feelings hurt.

Realizing that she had to change her behavior, she became willing to practice simple, honest communication skills even though, being new and unfamiliar, they made her feel uncomfortable. She says she has learned to speak the truth and to give an honest report of her feelings even at the risk of the other person perhaps not being ready to hear it.

She hastens to add, "That doesn't mean I have the right to give the same report over and over again. When I do that, it usually means I am trying to control the other person."

Mean what you say when you do the Third Step ("Made a decision to turn our will and our lives over to the care of God—*as we understood Him*")[1] and when you say the Third Step Prayer, ("God, I offer myself to Thee—to build with me and to do with me as Thou wilt. Relieve me of the bondage of self, that I may better do Thy will. Take away my difficulties that victory over them may bear witness to those I would help of Thy Power, Thy Love, and Thy Way of Life. May I do Thy will always!")[2]

People often complain bitterly, frequently, and at length about a problem, and have no idea how to get comfortable. They blame their job, their boss, their spouse, a fellow-employee, any one of the many things that commonly upset us. When questioned, they insist they've done all the Steps, and are usually emphatic about having specifically done the Third Step.

They forget, as I often do, that the decision of the Third Step constitutes a definite contract. The contract tells God to take control of our lives, and to do with us whatever He wants. Then we are unhappy and complain about what He has done. We act as if the things that are happening now are happening by mistake.

When I realize that I've forgotten about the contract, I know I must do one of two things: Either cancel the contract by retaking control of my life and getting God out of the driver's seat, or accept the fact that God is in charge of the situation and in His infinite wisdom has allowed things to evolve in precisely the way that they have.

---

[1] *Alcoholics Anonymous*, 3rd Ed., p. 59
[2] *Alcoholics Anonymous*, 3rd Ed., p. 63

If I choose the latter, I need to learn the lesson and move on with my life. Complaining gets me nowhere. The Third Step, as I see it, is a contract which must be lived, not mouthed meaninglessly.

I've always taken this Step seriously. I've told this story frequently. The first time I took the Third Step, I recited the Step and the Third Step Prayer on my knees with my sponsor as my witness. Later, in order to increase the number of witnesses, and thereby to make the contract more difficult to rescind, I repeated this process in front of my three home groups.

Still not satisfied, I decided that ideally a contract should be in writing. At a business supply store I picked up a blank form for establishing a Limited Partnership. I filled it out and gave God a 51% controlling interest in my life. He became the General Partner, and I made myself a Limited Partner.

But then I realized that that paper showed only the existence of a Limited Partnership. It said nothing about the terms of the partnership. So finally I listed our respective responsibilities, His and mine. Essentially, it narrowed down to the fact that I am in charge of work, and He is in charge of worry. And my experience has been that He doesn't like for me to even help Him with the worry, and He never does the slightest bit of the work.

Be realistic. Don't expect your partner to do the impossible. Don't expect him or her to give you something they don't have now, and never have had. Don't be like the gal who complained constantly that her drinking husband didn't give her the love and affection she needed. Her sponsor pointed out that her husband was full of hatred for himself. Furthermore, he'd been raised in a home where love and affection didn't exist. Obviously he couldn't give her something he didn't have. Her sponsor said she sounded like a person going to a hardware store to buy a loaf of bread, and then being angry because they didn't give it to her.

Rely on the Third Step prayer. If I do a thing for the right motive and leave the results up to God, things turns out the way they are supposed to turn out. I carry only half the equation, the easy half. I am responsible for my motive, for what prompts me to do what I do. I am not responsible for how things turn out.

Love is always a good motive. Commonly I have more than one motive, but I alone decide which is my main motive. It's my choice, not anyone else's. If, for example, being loving or carrying the message is my motive, and I leave the results up to God, things turn out the way they are meant to turn out. Life is much simpler this way. That's how I discover God's Will for me—by the way things turn out.

On the other hand, none of my prayers have ever convinced God that He should tell me ahead of time what He would do if I were to take a certain action. He will *not* reveal the future to me. It would be so much easier for me to make decisions if He would, but He never has.

Anyway, things seem to turn out the way they should in spite of me not knowing in advance. I'm reminded of a poster in my den that says, "If I'd gotten the job I wanted at Montgomery Ward, I suppose I would never have left Illinois." The author of that statement failed to get the job he wanted. Later he became a radio sports announcer, then a movie actor, president of the screen actors' union, a politician, governor of the State of California, and finally President of the United States. So, who knows?

Make a decision. Only rarely have I received unsolicited junk e-mail that I appreciated. An exception occurred once when someone sent me a story about a man waiting in an airport. While waiting, the man saw another man return home from a relatively short business trip. As he watched, the returnee was enthusiastically greeted by his wife and three children.

The joy, love and caring in the encounter was so obvious that the first man asked the couple how long they had been married. When told they had been married twelve years, he said, "Gee, I hope my marriage is still that passionate after twelve years!"

At this, he said the family man suddenly stopped smiling. "He looked me straight in the eye, and with forcefulness that burned right into my soul, he told me something that left me a different person. He told me, 'Don't *hope*, friend . . . . *Decide!*'"

At my thirtieth A.A. birthday party, a friend publicly announced that years earlier he had repeatedly called me complaining about an abusive relationship in which he was involved. He said I finally told him, "You're being abused, and you're whining about it. You have two choices: Either stop being abused or stop whining about it." He chose the former, and is currently in a very different and really beautiful relationship.

Many of us simply complain out of habit. If you find yourself complaining repeatedly about the same situation, it may be time to change something.

Several couples I know attend Al-Anon because of a wayward adult son or daughter. They've distanced themselves to some extent, but they continue to obsess over what their offspring might be doing or thinking. While a bit more comfortable than before they got into recovery, they remain unhappy and worried, and they show it. They accept their constant distress as "natural," and blame it on the fact that they "love him/her so much." Like many parents of the old-school, they feel guilty any time they feel the least bit happy while their son or daughter is still suffering. They think that by their misery they show their love for the wayward child. Their constant message is, "Notice how we suffer; see how much we love you."

Wouldn't both the parents and their offspring be better off if they, in a sense, divorced their child? Like so many parents before them, they could stop saying by their actions and their mood, "We can't be happy until you're happy too." The wayward adult-child could stop feeling guilty for allegedly making their parents unhappy, and everyone involved could get on with their life—and the alcoholic might even get sober!

It's natural to become upset when someone we love becomes embroiled in a serious personal problem, but it can be a trap. Like the couples above, we can end up "proving" our love by the depth of our distress. This adds to the total suffering caused by the problem and benefits no one.

Act like a winner. Bill W, one of the co-founders of AA, said that carrying the message of Alcoholics Anonymous is our primary aim and the chief reason for our existence. "Primary aim." "Chief reason for our existence." Those are strong words. And when he said "our existence," did he mean us as individuals or us as groups—or both?

If carrying the message is the chief reason for our existence, then, of the many ways of doing this, what could be better than acting in all our affairs like a winner, like a successful member of A.A.? Real winners portray the message in the way they conduct themselves in all their relationships including at work and at home—perhaps especially at home. Although winners don't compete with the people they sponsor, all too often we see these same people in intense, unconscious competition with their spouse or partner, the very person with whom they are trying to establish a loving relationship. Being a loving person is not compatible with the need to outsmart or control one's partner.

Cut It Short. Regrettably, things will crop up that upset us. In recovery, however, we don't let these things bother us for as long as they formerly did. Feeling good becomes more important than playing the victim role or punishing someone else by pouting. When we realize what is happening, we do whatever we need to do to not stay upset. We change our priorities. Whatever was upsetting us becomes less important than our emotional sobriety.

Otherwise, we act like my little dog Sabrina. There's a kindly old gentleman in our neighborhood who loves dogs, and had a dog that looked very much like Sabrina. For some reason, Sabrina hated that dog and always carried on at length whenever it came near.

The dog has been dead now for several years, and Sabrina is now blind. But she still hates that man because he had that dog, and she carries on every time she hears his voice. The other day, as we were about to pass on the sidewalk, I suggested that he not say anything and see if Sabrina knew he was nearby. She didn't. Because she didn't, the man laughed, and the minute Sabrina heard him laugh, she began to carry on like before.

Sabrina needs to talk to her sponsor; she carries a grudge much too far and too long.

Whine a little.   When Delores led the Al-Anon topic-discussion meeting, she asked us to talk about our favorite tool of the program. I immediately thought of whining. I hate whining when I'm being whined to, but, at least for a while, I enjoy it when I'm the whiner.

When speaking at an A.A. meeting, if I think of it, I give out my phone number and invite people to call me when they need to talk. One day a caller asked who I talk to when I have a problem. Without hesitation, I said, "The next person who calls." However, after I've done this several times, I hear myself sounding like a victim, and since I can't stand to hear people whine, I stop it.

Whining is kind of like worry in that they both seem to work for brief periods. They let us feel like we're doing something about our problem. Regrettably, we're actually putting energy into the problem rather than into the answer, and thereby keeping the problem alive.

Accept your partner's behavior. Sometimes I get annoyed at Max's behavior, and either consciously or unconsciously show it. I do this hoping she will notice my disapproval, feel responsible for my discomfort, and change the way she is acting. In childhood, this was called pouting, and it worked.

Now, however, instead of doing what I want her to do, Max does what I'm doing. She becomes annoyed at my behavior, and begins to show it. By showing it, she hopes I'll notice her disapproval and change my behavior.

Now we are both resentful and both focused on how the other ought to "shape up." We postpone our own happiness and insist the other must change before we will feel better. Their behavior is more important than our feelings.

Eventually, one of us changes our attitude. We accept the other as they are, and we accept responsibility for our own emotional state. As I said before, Max and I often end an episode like this by agreeing, "I'll put up with you if you'll put up with me."

Recently we were asked to lead and participate in a meeting of Couples in Recovery. Being an anniversary meeting, it was followed by a pot-luck. About ten of us sat at each table. Next to me sat a man sober ten months after an 18-month slip following 3 years of sobriety. Next to him sat his wife.

That's all she did. She sat like a statue. When he left to get more food, I tried to talk to her about Al-Anon. Although she wasn't attending, she said she'd "been to Al-Anon," and she made it obvious that she had no intention of returning in the near future. She answered questions with the minimum of words, spoke to no one else, had no eye contact with anyone and displayed a constant bored expression. Obviously she felt it her duty to pout. If she didn't, he'd think it was okay to drink and he'd do it again, right? Apparently she thought his sobriety was her responsibility, and it had to be dealt with in a serious, somber manner.

It's important to remember once again that acceptance is not approval. Acceptance does not mean approval any more than it means tolerating intolerable behavior. Physical violence, for example, may have to be accepted as a factual reality—but it is not to be tolerated.

Detach (Release). If someone offered a prize for the one word that best describes the Al-Anon program, I'd submit the word "detachment," sometimes referred to as "emotional detachment." Here in the western part of the country, this is often called release, or release with love. These are all good names, but emotional detachment has the additional implication of detaching only emotionally and only from the problem—not from the person.

No matter what they call it, when you are released, especially early in recovery, it feels like rejection. However, in spite of the negative feeling, this is an important time for both the releasee—the one being released, and for the releasor—the one doing the releasing. This is an indication that the whole family has begun to recover.

A simple, brief example of emotional detachment is illustrated by the statement of an Al-Anon mother who was doing what was best for her family rather than what they wanted her to do. To her drug-using children and alcoholic husband she said, "It's more important that I be a good mother than that you like me."

A more elaborate story is that of Sue W., mentioned earlier, who had considerable trouble releasing her husband. Sue told me she and he were almost fatally enmeshed, both at home and in his professional office where she took over as manager. She said their relationship was based on so much chaos and turmoil that to have it otherwise seemed not only impossible but a little boring. She played the role of victim and he the aggressor. She felt abused and in turn became abusive. Each knew the other's buttons and stayed focused on their partner's inappropriate behavior. Not only was Sue afraid to look at her part in what was going on, she was afraid to give up trying to control with its false sense of importance.

Sue says she initially went to Al-Anon simply to justify later getting a divorce. Her first year was, she said, the most difficult of her life. Among other things, she had to, without going to his rescue, watch him make what she thought were mistakes. Worst of all, she had to give up her self image of a self-sacrificing wife and mother who put everyone else's life and needs ahead of her own. Then she had to find out who she really was, and what she herself wanted out of life. This required participation in many meetings and active involvement in both A.A. and Al-Anon. She says she now realizes that happiness really is an inside job.

Here's one of the things Al-Anon[3] has to say about detaching:

> What does another person's mood, tone of voice or state of inebriation have to do with my course of actions? Nothing, unless I decide otherwise.
>
> For example, I have learned that arguing with someone who is intoxicated is like beating my head against a brick wall. Yet, until recently, I would always dive right into the arguments, because that was what the other person seemed to want. In Al-Anon I discovered that I don't have to react just because I have been provoked, and I don't have to take harsh words to heart. I can remember that they are coming from someone who may be in pain, and try to show a little compassion. I certainly don't have to allow them to provoke me into anything I don't want to do.
>
> Today's reminder: Detachment with love means that I stop depending upon what others do, say, or feel to determine my own well-being or to make my decisions. When faced with other people's destructive attitudes and behavior, I can love their best, and never fear their worst.

_____

[3] *Courage to Change*, p. 72

"Detachment is not caring less, it's caring more for my own serenity."

...In All Our Affairs

Be an interested observer. Have you ever watched the continuing deterioration of someone you really want to help? A close relative or friend, say, or one or more of your children, and they don't respond to anything you say or do?

This can be particularly frustrating and discouraging for people in recovery. You want so badly to help, but you can't. They just don't hear you. They don't respond to any of your (usually unsolicited) advice or counsel.

This happens to me when I try too hard in sponsoring, when I find that I'm working harder on their recovery than they are. It also happens to people who want to be one of those highly directive, dictatorial type sponsors, but lack the appropriate personality for the job, and their sponsees simply ignore them.

In situations like this, I assume the role of interested observer. Rather than becoming annoyed at them and at sponsorship in general, I become an interested but inactive observer. I listen. I'm interested in what they are doing and wonder how the story will end. I may answer an occasional question or make an innocuous comment, but mainly I observe.

I picture myself sitting quietly in the audience rather than as projected into the action on the screen. I find the story fascinating, but I'm not personally involved in how it turns out. Having no personal investment in the outcome, I'm not involved in making it come out my way. It's like watching an interesting movie.

As a result, I'm comfortable and entertained rather than frustrated and resentful. Indeed, I'm practicing the A.A. principle, *Love and tolerance of others is our code.*[4] And one more time I realize that if I want to change my feelings, I must first change my actions and my thinking—mine, not theirs. I can not let their behavior be more important to me than my emotional sobriety, my serenity. No matter how much I love them, no matter how much I care about them, no matter how important their welfare is to me, I must watch my priorities. I must value my serenity ahead of their behavior.

It has been my pleasure to watch many program people benefit by adopting this approach. Here in her own words is what Jayne U. says about the interested observer role:

> I have a large family that has been much affected by the disease of alcoholism. It seems that someone is always in a crisis or has a problem. Because I'm in recovery and like to think I've learned a great deal about life and problem solving, I thought it my duty to share my wisdom and knowledge with whoever came to me. I also thought that I had to help. I did this with time, advice and/or money. I was always surprised when my time and money were taken, but

---

[4] *Alcoholics Anonymous*, 3rd Ed., p. 84.

never my advice. But I kept on trying to make it better. I also spent a great deal of time worrying and being afraid for them.

I found myself feeling bitter and resentful toward my family. My life in recovery would be so great if only they would shape up and leave me alone! What a blessing it has been for me to learn about being an interested observer. I can be a part of their lives without the need to fix or protect them. This leaves me free to be close and loving and to enjoy their company. I can even laugh at some to their antics. What a relief!

Daily, I put myself and my loved ones in God's care, then I get busy living this wonderful gift that is life.

Keep it Light. In addition to the role of interested observer, do what you can to keep it light. The other person is probably taking himself far too seriously. Stay interested and empathic, but don't get carried away with the seriousness of the situation.

Here's a story you might not consider humorous, but it's true, and it worked for me. A man called at 9:30 in the evening. It was after midnight back where he was. He said he was in a hospital bed, was two weeks post open-heart surgery and had lost his health, wife, family, job and money. He said, "I've got four drugs in me right now, but I haven't drunk yet." Then he repeated what he had said. He had been listening to a tape of one of my talks during which I had given my phone number. He was calling to tell me he'd decided that he might as well kill himself. In addition, he went on in great detail about how he quoted me so often on acceptance and page 449 that people were tired of listening to him.

I let him go on at length about his plans. Then I agreed that suicide was definitely an option. Indeed, suicide is the ultimate option available to each of us. I pointed out, however, that it has a major flaw in that when we use it, we automatically use up all our other options.

I said I could readily see how he could come to the conclusion to kill himself, but I asked that if he did decide to do so, would he, for God's sake, please, please, please, not tell anyone that he had called me first! There was more at stake, I pointed out, than just his life. My reputation should be considered. I'd worked on it for a very long time, and he could now ruin it in an instant.

I also mentioned that I had heard on the best authority that however one feels when they kill themselves, that's how they're going to feel for all of eternity. So, obviously one should never kill oneself on a bad day.

He started laughing. The next morning he called while I was walking the dog and told Max to tell me everything had changed, he felt fine now and thanks very much.

Change. Change what? Many of us come into recovery not having gotten the changes we wanted because we sought to change the wrong person. Ask any marriage counselor, and they'll tell you that most couples seeking help want their partner to change.

Ultimately we come to realize that, as difficult as it is to change ourselves, it's easier than changing someone else. Furthermore, while it's basically impossible by force of will to change our personalities, it's relatively easy to change our attitudes. The Serenity Prayer could in fact be modified to: God grant me either the ability to change this situation or the courage to change my attitude toward it.

Naomi, who told us a bit of her story earlier, had to change a habit that went back to her childhood. She told me that after twelve years in her current marriage and two marriages to men with entirely different personalities, she faced her second divorce.

In doing her inventory work, she learned that she had said yes twice to marriages when she didn't feel comfortable doing so. She discovered that giving her power away in this manner was an unhealthy pattern that she had developed in childhood. She knew people were disappointed in her when she didn't do what they wanted her to do, and she felt responsible for their feelings. She wanted to fix them. As a child, always giving her power to her mother in order to please her felt good because it made her feel wanted and loved. But now, as an adult, it wasn't working.

Today, she says that although she occasionally finds it hard to not try to fix their disappointment, she gives people the right to be disappointed in her. If they try to make her feel guilty for not doing what they want by telling her they are disappointed in her, she tells them, "Yes, I know. I'm disappointed in me too. It happens all the time."

An answer like that is a good example of assertiveness. It's not passively submitting, and it's not aggressively fighting or arguing; it's the honest truth.

In order to speak assertively, one must feel a certain degree of self-confidence. On the other hand, my personal experience has been that self-confidence develops as a direct result of speaking assertively. While it seems risky at first, it soon becomes a most comfortable way of talking to others.

9. NOW SIMPLIFY

My mind is like a powerful laser beam or search light which locks on to all sorts of impractical ideas. It has a mind of its own, and like the parent of an adolescent at a computer, I must periodically check on what it is doing. If left alone too long, it thinks all kinds of impractical, illegal, lewd or ridiculous thoughts. It tries to solve unsolvable problems, or problems I didn't know I had, or win debates with people who aren't even present.

On the other hand, some of my best ideas show up on just such occasions. An example would be my theory as to the cause of alcoholism as described in my previous book, *There's More to Quitting Drinking than Quitting Drinking.* No one knows the cause of alcoholism. Every explanation you hear, no matter from how distinguished a source, is just a theory, a guess. That being so, I have the right to reject any theory I don't care for, and a perfect right to make up my own.

I like my theory. It says alcoholics generate a great deal of love—whether they want to or not, and perhaps especially if they don't want to. But they lack the ability to express love. Since they can't express love, can't give it away, it builds up like the pressure in a tea kettle. This causes discomfort. They drink to suppress this discomfort, and they feel better for the moment. However, their drinking compounds the already existing communication problem.

Not only can alcoholics not express love, they can't accept love. They can't allow themselves to be loved. As a result, people who love them can't express their love, and they end up with essentially the same pressure problem. They become increasingly more uncomfortable as the emotional tension builds up. They can find no relief. Their feelings must come out, but can't be expressed as love, so they come out as anger, frustration, resentment, hostility, even violence and other negative emotions.

This, of course, doesn't solve the problem. It makes the situation worse by further compounding the basic communication problem, and now both partners are emotionally disturbed.

There's nothing anyone can do about a situation like this. So, what happens? If they're lucky, they end up as newcomers—the alcoholic in A.A., and the spouse, relative or friend in Al-Anon.

What do we do with newcomers? We love the hell out of them. We literally love the hell out of their hellish lives. And we teach them, by example, how to express love.

We don't call it love. Like talking about God, that might scare newcomers away. We love them by making them feel important. They are important to us for these three reasons: Alcoholism is a disease, the A.A. and Al-Anon programs are a spiritual answer to that disease, and we have to give that answer away in order to keep it. The more we give it away, the more we get to keep it. We need newcomers—for our own benefit as much as for theirs.

Love has been defined as an *active* concern for another person's welfare. It has also been defined (my favorite definition) as *making the other person feel important.* We make the newcomer feel important by treating them with respect and by showing them how important they really are. We do this when we make them feel welcome, remember their names, smile at them, are attentive, and in so many, many other big and little ways.

The newcomer responds to this attention, this love. The alcoholic newcomer stops drinking, and the Al-Anon member begins to recover. They don't even realize what is happening. Then, following our example, they begin to treat people newer than themselves with the same care and respect. They practice love without realizing what they are doing. They've learned to both accept and express love by following our example.

Love *vs* fear. I like this theory about alcoholism, not only because it's mine, but because it fits so well into the belief, mentioned earlier, that there are only two basic emotions: love and fear. All other emotions are variations of one or the other of these two.

This concept first came to my attention in *A Course In Miracles*[1] and later in the much more readable *Love Is Letting Go Of Fear*[2] by Jampolski.

Limiting the choices to only two basic emotions really simplifies life. I can respond to life either with fear or with love. Prior to sobriety, I did what I did because I was afraid not to do it, and I didn't do

---

[1] *A Course In Miracles*, (Glen Elen, CA: Foundation For Inner Peace, 1975).

[2] G.G. Jampolski, *Love Is Letting Go of Fear*, rev. ed. (Berkeley, CA: Celestial Arts, 1988).

things I wanted to do because I was afraid to do them. I lived a fear-based life.

In recovery, I base my actions as much as possible on love rather than on fear. I remind myself that I am most comfortable when I do a thing for the right motive (and love is always a right motive), and leave the results up to God. Under these circumstances, things turn out the way they are supposed to.

The main problem with this theory of only two emotions is that it seems unrealistic, too good to be livable. Yet I haven't found it so. Over the years I've met a number of couples who fought most of the time until one of them decided to live life according to this concept. The one who made the decision began to respond in love rather than in fear and refused to fight under any circumstances.

When reacting in love became more important than winning, fear of losing disappeared. In the end, they and their partner both won. When one stopped fighting (stopped reacting in fear), the other (sooner or later) followed suit. It's truly remarkable the extent to which one partner can become a role model, can have such a positive influence on a relationship.

As someone once said, love conquers all. While constantly reacting in love may seem like an impossible goal, as someone (I don't know who) said, "Goals are like stars; we may not reach them, but like mariners on the sea, we chart our course by them."

Acting out of love instead of fear can seem particularly impractical in dealing with our immediate families, perhaps especially with teen-agers. Fearing that they won't turn out right, we react in fear.

This was abruptly brought to the attention of a friend of mine, a single-parent father. Following one of his very vocal "now-I'm-telling-you-for-the-last-time" lectures, his fifteen year old daughter, as she slammed her bedroom door, yelled out, "I wish you'd treat me the way you treat the people you sponsor!"

This concept of only two basic emotions, love and fear, seems particularly appropriate for marriage counseling. In many situations with which I am familiar, either both members of the partnership are strong-willed, or one is strong-willed and the other is passive-aggressive—that is, agrees to everything, but changes nothing.

Such couples commonly end up in a power struggle with each partner determined to win. When consulting a therapist, they often put that person in the role of manager, coach, contract negotiator or score keeper who makes suggestions regarding possible contracts. "Now if she agrees to do what you want in this matter, then you agree to let her have her way in this other matter. Is that right? Are we all in agreement on this?" This is negotiating in fear. I'll give up a little of my fear (of losing) if you'll give up a little of yours.

In my experience, the really successful negotiations are those in which one partner says, in effect, "I love you as you are. I am not going to leave you. I want to live the rest of my life with you. Your happiness is important to me. From now on, I am not going to fight you or try to change you."

How do you get to where you can make such a statement? Years ago I heard Johnnie A. say at a meeting that, when uncertain as to what to do next, he asks himself, "What is the loving thing to do? What would God want me to do?"

Admittedly, in the middle of an argument or debate, such a question requires a drastic change in one's thinking. On the other hand, a change is often precisely what is needed, and, while I wish I remembered to ask the question more often, I have found that it becomes easier with practice.

When either partner takes this approach to marital harmony, the other is able to change without losing face, without having the feeling of having been forced to change. Both partners win. Nobody loses.

In my experience, one of the simplest and easiest times to practice this loving approach is when your partner has become upset, but you haven't yet lost your sense of calm. My natural inclination when faced with negative emotions is to immediately react in kind. Of course, the loving thing to do is to listen and learn, and to not join them in their disturbed emotional state.

Naturally, some behavior on the part of a partner is easier to accept than others. All sorts of examples exist. Chronic lack of sexual gratification can be particularly galling—especially when such denial is used as a weapon. It's also unpleasant when our spouse, family, kids, neighbors, friends, employers or others treat us unfairly or in a demeaning manner. It's difficult to not let these things control our emotions—at least temporarily. Handling such predicaments require a great deal of prayer and meditation combined with strenuous efforts to learn and practice effective communicating skills.

Acceptance, of course, is the final answer. Eventually one accepts the situation as unchangeable and gets on with one's life—without resentment. One accepts the reality of the situation and then either leaves and is comfortable in being free of it, or stays and is comfortable in having made the decision to stay. The real trick is to not vacillate and to not hold on to the resentment that caused the fear and the power struggle in the first place.

Regarding fear, one of our most pervasive fears is the fear of being found out, of having our innermost secrets exposed. Early in sobriety I remember hearing a woman say she was so depressed she would kill herself if it weren't for the fact she "would be killing the wrong person." Before she died she wanted someone to look inside and see the real person there, but she was afraid to let them look for fear they'd see what she didn't want them to see.

In the program, we hear the statement, "We are as sick as our secrets." This came to mind a short while ago when they removed the top of my right ear because of skin cancer. I was scheduled to speak at a meeting two days after surgery and wanted to hide my ear. At a surgical supply store I looked for bandages specifically for covering an ear. I tried on one dressing after another while asking Max which was less obvious. Finally, I realized I had a secret. I was trying to hide my self from my peers.

As a little time passed and the pain in my ear subsided, I forgot that I had an ear. Without benefit of a mirror, I couldn't even see my ear. That being the case, my ear wasn't my problem. If anyone's problem, it was yours to handle any way you wanted. I was free to forget it.

Attitude. All of what we have been talking about, all of life for that matter, is a question of attitude. Nothing is more importance than our ongoing attitude toward ourselves, others, and life in general. The so-called Law of Appreciation tells us that here on earth, nothing, no thing and no person, is perfect. Every person, place, thing, situation, circumstance, organization, law, institution or whatever has both good and bad in it. If there is a heaven, perhaps everything there will be totally good, and in hell everything will be totally bad. But here on earth we must accept this combination of both good and bad.

Because of this co-existence of both positive and negative, people who smile, always have something to smile about; and people who complain, always have something to complain about. They are both right. Each is exercising their choice as to what to look at.

The Law of Appreciation also tells us our thoughts have energy. When we focus that energy on the good, the good gets better. When we focus on the bad, the bad gets worse. Check this out for yourself. I've found it to be true in my life as it relates to my relationship with Max and all my relationships, both personal and impersonal.

Happiness is an attitude, and our attitudes are our responsibility, no one else's. Our happiness depends on our communications within ourselves, with others and with God. Others treat us the way we teach them to treat us. Any change in our relationships as far as communication is concerned must begin with us.

In an attempt to improve my communication with my Higher Power, I've recently been modifying the Serenity Prayer. I say, *God, grant me the serenity to calmly accept the things I cannot change, the courage to change my attitude, and the wisdom to enjoy life's journey.*

One more suggestion—sometimes both the hardest and the easiest of all: Pray with your partner.

I don't understand why I found it difficult. Max has seen me naked. She has seen me having a convulsion. She has seen me lying on the floor having wet myself and unable to get up. Yet for some reason I was uncomfortable having her see me on my knees talking to God.

After several men in our stag group talked about the remarkable benefit they experienced as a result of praying regularly with their spouse, I decided to try it. It worked and it continues to work. Try it out yourself.

There are many ways of doing it. Currently we recite the Serenity Prayer and the Third and Seventh Step Prayers (see Appendix V, page 95.) Then we read a page from Al-Anon's *One Day at a Time* and *Courage to Change*. After thus setting the tone, I talk aloud to God about the sort of things I ordinarily include in my automatic writing to Him. I express my gratitude and let Him know where I stand with what's going on down here. I ask for the removal of certain of my character defects, and request that he look with favor on specific people and especially on some whose behavior I do not like. There's no rigid routine. Then Max talks to Him in a similar manner.

As a result, Max and I get to know and understand each other better. The results are well worth the time and trouble. I highly recommend a practice of this type—whether or not things are currently going well.

Goals. Earlier we talked about goals. I'm much clearer on my goals today than I was as a young boy. At that time, while others seemed to know what they were doing and were apparently succeeding at doing it, I couldn't see the point. Where are we headed? I wondered. What are we trying to do? What are the rules?

Later, as an adolescent, the goal seemed to be to get through this life, this "vale of tears" as they called it, and get to heaven. The purpose of being here was to end up there. Life ended on one final crap shoot. Everything depended on one's state of grace at the moment of death. This meant two choices: Either live a fun-filled life of sin and beg forgiveness at the precise moment of death, or live like a saint and don't die while sinning.

Then, as a young adult, accumulation of wealth seemed to be the goal. The person dying with the biggest pile of "stuff" was the winner. I didn't find this particularly satisfying. For one thing, I lacked the "smarts" needed to win. I also had doubts about the whole thing.

I don't particularly care for greeting cards, but many years ago I received one that had a profound effect on me. It said material wealth didn't matter. What really mattered, it said, was the number of people whose lives had benefited by the fact that you had lived. I interpreted that as requiring doing something like winning the Nobel Prize in medicine. I didn't have the "smarts" for that either.

Eventually I ended up in the nut ward of a hospital where I was a member of the medical staff. As if that wasn't bad enough, they sent me to A.A. There the goal was simply to not drink. They insisted if you don't drink today, you're a success today.

As a life goal, that struck me as embarrassingly simplistic and ridiculously inadequate. (I was still drinking at the time.) My own goals and good intentions had always been something of which I was quite proud. I considered myself one of the best-intentioned people I knew. I'd be happy to match mine against yours any time.

But then, during my second year in A.A., I suddenly realized that if I couldn't succeed at such a humble, seemingly insignificant goal as A.A.'s daily sobriety goal, I'd never succeed at anything. Nothing whatsoever. Eventually, becoming a lifelong, successful member of A.A. became my life goal, and the A.A. spiritual way of life became my road map.

As a result, I now have both a simple, specific, attainable goal and simple, specific directions for achieving it.

Along that line, Bill W., as mentioned earlier in Chapter 7, said that carrying A.A.'s message of recovery was our primary goal and the chief reason for our existence. According to Bill, staying sober and carrying the message of recovery to others is the most important things we can do.

I used to fantasize about receiving the Nobel Prize for having discovered the cure for an important, worldwide medical problem. I planned, upon receiving the Prize, to give all the credit to God. I was going to make God famous. All I asked was that He make me famous first. That wasn't asking too much. He already knew the answers I needed. All He had to do was give them to me. Then I'd travel around the country giving lectures on the diagnosis and treatment of the disease He'd told me about.

Today, I see that that is what He has done. I, along with millions of other alcoholics, have a disease, a medical problem. Most of the alcoholics throughout the world die for lack of knowledge of the things we regularly talk about in our meetings. But as a result of having this disease, I have, through the Grace of God and A.A., found a way of life that keeps my disease under complete and total control, and provides a better approach to life than anything I have ever known. Because of Alcoholics Anonymous, alcoholics get better than they were before they got sick; they get better than well. And by traveling about the country talking about my disease and my recovery, I am actually doing what I had always dreamed of doing as a physician. And, according to Dr. Bob, the other co-founder of A.A., the whole A.A. program can be expressed in the words "love and service."

To these simple, basic concepts, add the idea of emotional independence, and then add the idea that there are only two primary emotions, Love and Fear. You can't put life in a much simpler package than that.

10. THE END

Well, that's it. That's all there is. As in writing a Fourth Step, no doubt more could be written, but that's all that comes to mind at this time. This is as good a place to end as any. It's time to apply this stuff. Merely reading it, a half-measure, accomplishes nothing. Your communication skills will not improve. Remember the story told earlier about the man in the airport who said you must *decide*. Then you must *do* it.

On the other hand, if you picked up only one or two communication skills, or just one idea, or maybe only the title, and if you practice diligently, it may turn out to be well worth your time and trouble.

I hope so.

But for heaven's sake, don't let anything I've said upset you. That would be a complete negation of everything the book is about!

Writing this has been good for me. If it didn't do much for you, do your own writing on the same subject. It will make you think. Writing about emotional independence and emotional sobriety will keep them in your mind, and you can't practice something if you don't remember it. We have to intentionally hold the thought until it becomes an unconscious habit. This is one of the ways in which writing has helped me.

If you did get something out of this book, and you want more, there are all kinds of books and other sources of information on the subject of interpersonal communications. Remember that life—especially interpersonal relationships—is essentially a communication problem. If you have comfortable, joyful, effective communication with the voices in your head, with your Higher Power, and with the people in your life, especially those closest to you, you will have a comfortable, joyful, effective life.

I wish you happy, ongoing recovery. Enjoy life. Remember, that's really what we're here for.

We absolutely insist on enjoying life.[1]

THE END

---

[1] *Alcoholics Anonymous*, 3rd Ed., p. 132.

Appendix I

The A.A. Preamble

[The A.A. Grapevine, Inc.]*

Alcoholics Anonymous is a fellowship of men and women who share their experience, strength and hope with each other that they may solve their common problem and help others to recover from alcoholism. The only requirement for membership is a desire to stop drinking. There are no dues or fees for A.A. membership; we are self-supporting through our own contributions. A.A. is not allied with any sect, denomination, politics, organization or institution; does not wish to engage in any controversy; neither endorses nor opposes any causes. Our primary purpose is to stay sober and help other alcoholics to achieve sobriety.

---

* 475 Riverside Dr., New York, NY , 10115.

Appendix II
The Twelve Steps of Alcoholics Anonymous
[*Alcoholics Anonymous*, Ed 3, pg 59]

1. We admitted we were powerless over alcohol—that our lives had become unmanageable.
2. Came to believe that a Power greater than ourselves could restore us to sanity.
3. Made a decision to turn our will and our lives over to the care of God *as we understood Him.*
4. Made a searching and fearless inventory of ourselves.
5. Admitted to God, to ourselves, and to another human being the exact nature of our wrongs.
6. Were entirely ready to have God remove all these defects of character.
7. Humbly asked Him to remove our shortcomings.
8. Made a list of all persons we had harmed and became willing to make amends to them all.
9. Made direct amends to such people wherever possible, except when to do so would injure them or others.
10. Continued to take personal inventory and when we were wrong promptly admitted it.
11. Sought through prayer and meditation to improve our conscious contract with God *as we understood Him*, praying only for knowledge of His will for us and the power to carry that out.
12. Having had a spiritual awakening as the result of these steps, we tried to carry this message to alcoholics, and to practice these principles in all our affairs.

Appendix III
Suggested Al-Anon/Alateen Welcome
[*How Al-anon Works*, p. 8]

We welcome you to the Al-Anon Family Groups and hope you will find in this fellowship the help and friendship we have been privileged to enjoy. We who live or have lived with the problem of alcoholism understand as perhaps few others can. We, too, were lonely and frustrated, but in Al-Anon we discover that no situation is really hopeless, and that it is possible for us to find contentment and even happiness, whether the alcoholic is still drinking or not.

We urge you to try our program. It has helped many of us find solutions that lead to serenity. So much depends on our own attitudes, and as we learn to place our problem in its true perspective, we find that it loses its power to dominate our thoughts and our lives.

The family situation is bound to improve as we apply the Al-Anon ideas. Without such spiritual help, living with an alcoholic is too much for most of us. Our thinking becomes distorted by trying to force solutions, and we become irritable and unreasonable without knowing it.

The Al-Anon program is based on the Twelve Steps (adapted from Alcoholics Anonymous) which we try, little by little, one day at a time, to apply to our lives along with our slogans and the Serenity Prayer. The loving interchange of help among members and daily reading of Al-Anon literature thus make us ready to receive the priceless gift of serenity.

Al-Anon is an anonymous fellowship. Everything that is said here, in the group meeting and member-to-member, must be held in confidence. Only in this way can we feel free to say what is in our minds and hearts, for this is how we help one another in Al-Anon.

Appendix IV
Understanding Ourselves
[*Understanding Ourselves and Alcoholism*, Al-Anon pamphlet
P-48]

Alcoholism is a "family" disease. Compulsive drinking affects the drinker and it affects the drinker's relationships; friendships, employment, childhood, parenthood, love affairs, marriages, all suffer from the effects of alcoholism. Those special relationships in which a person is really close to an alcoholic are affected most, and the people who *care* are the most caught up in the behavior of another person. They react to an alcoholic's behavior. They see that the drinking is out of hand and they try to control it. They are ashamed of the public scenes but in private they try to handle it. It isn't long before they feel they are to blame and take on the hurts, the fears, the guilt of an alcoholic.

These well-meaning people begin to count the number of drinks another person is having. They pour expensive liquor down drains, search the house for hidden bottles, listen for the sound of opening cans. All their thinking is directed at what the alcoholic is doing or not doing and how to get the drinker to stop drinking. This is their *obsession*.

Watching other human beings slowly kill themselves with alcohol is painful. While alcoholics don't seem to worry about the bills, the job, the children, the condition of their health, the people around them begin to worry. They make the mistake of covering up. They fix everything, make excuses, tell little lies to mend damaged relationships, and they worry some more. This is their *anxiety*.

Sooner or later the alcoholic's behavior makes other people angry. They realize that the alcoholic is not taking care of responsibilities, is telling lies, using them. They have begun to feel that the alcoholic doesn't love them and they want to strike back, punish, make the alcoholic pay for the hurt and frustration caused by uncontrolled drinking. This is their *anger*.

Those who are close to the alcoholic begin to pretend. They accept promises, they believe, they want to believe the problem has gone away each time there is a sober period. When every good sense tells them there is something wrong with the alcoholic's drinking and thinking, they still hide how they feel and what they know. This is their *denial*.

Perhaps the most severe damage to those who have shared some part of life with an alcoholic comes in the form of the nagging belief that they are somehow at fault; they were not up to it all, not attractive enough, not clever enough to have solved this problem for the one they love. They think it was something they did or did not do. These are their *feelings of guilt*.

We, who have turned to Al-Anon, have often done so in despair, unable to believe in the possibility of change, unable to go on as we have before. We feel cheated out of a loving companion, over burdened with responsibilities, unwanted, unloved, and alone. There are even those of us who are arrogant, smug, self-righteous and dominating; but we come because we want, we need—help.

While we may have been driven to Al-Anon by the behavior of an alcoholic friend, spouse or child, a brother, sister or parent, we soon come to know that our own thinking has to change before we can make a new and successful approach to the problem of living. It is in Al-Anon that we learn to deal with our obsession, our anxiety, our anger, our denial, and our feelings of guilt. It is through the fellowship that we ease our emotional burdens by sharing our experience, strength and hope with others. Little by little, we come to realize at our meetings that much of our discomfort comes from our attitudes. We try to change these attitudes, learn about our responsibilities to ourselves, discover feelings of self-worth, love, and grow spiritually. The emphasis begins to be lifted from the alcoholics and placed where we do have some power—over our own lives.

Appendix V

Serenity Prayer
(*Alcoholics Anonymous Comes of Age*, pg. 196)

God, grant me the serenity to accept the things I cannot change, the courage to change the things I can, and the wisdom to know the difference.

Third Step Prayer
(*Alcoholics Anonymous*, 3rd ed., pg. 63)

God, I offer myself to Thee—to build with me and to do with me as Thou wilt. Relieve me of the bondage of self, that I may better do Thy will. Take away my difficulties that victory over them may bear witness to those I would help of Thy Power, Thy Love, and Thy Way of Life. May I do Thy will always!

Seventh Step Prayer
(*Alcoholics Anonymous*, 3rd ed., pg. 76)

My Creator, I am now willing that you should have all of me, good and bad. I pray that you now remove from me every single defect of character which stands in the way of my usefulness to you and my fellows. Grant me strength, as I go out from here, to do your bidding. Amen.

About the author:

From the time of his recovery in July of 1967 until his passing in May 2000, Dr. Paul was a tireless carrier of A.A.'s message. His story appeared in the 3rd edition of A.A.'s Big Book as "Doctor, Alcoholic, Addict" and included on page 449, "*And acceptance is the answer to all my problems today.*" This simple but powerful wisdom is quoted in twelve-step meetings around the world. It is regularly passed along from sponsors to newcomers, and shared between friends over coffee in the meetings-after-the-meeting. It has become such a fundamental philosophy that the 4th edition of the Big Book re-titled Dr. Paul's story as "Acceptance Was The Answer." (The quote appears on page 417 of the 4th edition of the Big Book.)

In addition to being a popular speaker at thousands of A.A. meetings, conventions and workshops, Dr. Paul was always willing to talk with fellow alcoholics. The phone in his home in Laguna Niguel, California would ring at all hours of the day and night. He also wrote the book "*There's More to Quitting Drinking than Quitting Drinking*" and edited and distributed the pamphlet, "*An Unofficial Guide to the Twelve Steps.*" To Dr. Paul, these were labors of love through which he could 'carry the message.'

He was the true embodiment of the AA Grapevine's Responsibility Declaration: "When anyone, anywhere, reaches out for help, I want the hand of AA always to be there. And for that: I am responsible."

NOTES

NOTES

NOTES

NOTES

NOTES

NOTES